Happy Selling!

☺ Debbie Mrazek

THE FIELD GUIDE TO SALES

THE ALL WEATHER, ALL TERRAIN GUIDE TO SELLING!

Bee Press

MRAZEK
The Sales Company

DEBBIE MRAZEK

# THE FIELD GUIDE TO SALES
THE ALL WEATHER, ALL TERRAIN GUIDE TO SELLING!
DEBBIE MRAZEK

Copyright © 2008
Bee Press. All rights reserved.
Published by Bee Press, Plano, Texas.

No part of this publication may be reproduced, stored in a retrieval system, or transmitted in any form or by any means, electronic, mechanical, photocopying, recording, scanning, or otherwise, except as permitted under Section 107 or 108 of the 1976 United States Copyright Act, without the prior written permission of the Publisher. Requests to the Publisher for permission should be addressed to Permissions Department, Bee Press, 7325 Paul Calle Drive, Plano, TX, 75025.

Limit of Liability/Disclaimer of Warranty: While the publisher and author have used their best efforts in preparing this book, they make no representations or warranties with respect to the accuracy or completeness of the contents of this book and specifically disclaim any implied warranties of merchantability or fitness for a particular purpose. No warranty may be created or extended by sales representatives or written sales materials. The advice and strategies contained herein may not be suitable for your situation. You should consult with a professional where appropriate. Neither the publisher nor author shall be liable for any loss of profit or any other commercial damages, including but not limited to special, incidental, consequential, or other damages.

ISBN: 978-0-9800428-0-1
Copyeditor: Christine Frank, www.ChristineFrank.com
Index: Christine Frank, www.ChristineFrank.com
Cover and Interior design: Toolbox Creative, www.ToolboxCreative.com

Library of Congress Cataloging-in-Publication Data
Library of Congress Control Number: 2007940209
Debbie Mrazek
The Field Guide to Sales
The All Weather, All Terrain Guide to Selling
www.TheFieldGuideToSales.com
ISBN: 978-0-9800428-0-1
2008

DEDICATIONS

Terry "The Tank" Pritchett
Age 25: Thought he was a tyrant for being so demanding!
Age 50: Realize he was a GENIUS!

✝

Rick Smith
1957-2007
My greatest competitor EVER!

Thank you for making the GAME OF SALES so much fun! Game over...much too soon. Look for me when I hit the lobby to the pearly gates...I will be wearing that power RED! Game ON...Round 2!

TABLE OF CONTENTS

PREFACE   9

INTRODUCTION   13

CHAPTER 1   17
FORECAST: YOUR MAP TO SUCCESS

You Need a Map	18
Don't Leave Home Without It	19
You Don't Have Time NOT to Forecast	20
Welcome to The Trailhead	21
Building Your Forecast, Step-by-Step	22
Timing is Everything	24
Prioritize with Success in Mind	25
Put your Forecast to Work	26
Use the Forecast as an Early Warning System	27

CHAPTER 2   33
YOUR ITINERARY

How Will You Spend the Next 168 Hours?	34
How Much Time Do You Really Have?	36
Changing Your View of Time	37
Customers Have Expectations About	
How You Should Spend Your Time	39
The Shortest Distance Between Two Points	41
Lifestyle = "Salestyle"	42

CHAPTER 3 — 47
YOUR BACKPACK & PROVISIONS

Get your Bearings	48
Become Familiar with Your Surroundings	48
Get to Know the Locals	49
Double-check Your Supply List	50
Do You Hear an Echo?	51
A Word about Attitude	52
Sore Muscles	53
One Foot in Front of the Other	54

CHAPTER 4 — 61
THE LANDSCAPE

Your Expectations of Yourself	62
Your Expectations of Your Customers	64
Your Expectations of Your Company and Coworkers	65
What Customers and Prospects Expect of You.	68
Expectations That Lead to Repeat Business	70
Your Company's Expectations of You	71
Your Coworkers' Expectations of You	72

CHAPTER 5 — 77
YOUR TRAVELING COMPANIONS

YOU Are What You Sell	78
YOU Are What They Buy	78
Getting There From Here	79
That First Step is a Doozey	80
Hire a Trail Guide	82

CHAPTER 6 — 89
OUTBOUND COMMUNICATIONS

Take the Lead	90
Moving Forward	92
What Makes You So Special?	92
Body Language	94
Follow the Scent of Opportunity	95
Back Away From the Scent of Skunks	96
Everyone Paddle! (in the Same Direction)	97

CHAPTER 7 — 103
INBOUND COMMUNICATION

Ready, Set, Sshhhhhhhh…	105
The Four Types of Listeners	108
Give and Let Give	109
Tune Your Receiver to the Strongest Signal	111

CHAPTER 8 — 117
AWARENESS OF THE ENVIRONMENT

A Great Set of Binoculars	118
Client Awareness	119
Industry/Competitor Awareness	122
Internal Company Awareness	123
Self-awareness	126

CHAPTER 9 — 133
CREATIVITY WINS THE DAY

Put Some Madness in your Method	134
An Open Mind Opens Doors	136
Energize Your Environment	137
The World is Your Oyster	138

CHAPTER 10 — 145
GETTING WHAT YOU CAME FOR

Don't Slip and Fall — 147
So What Brings You Here? — 148
Persistence = Payoff — 151
The Other Side of the Mountain — 152

CHAPTER 11 — 157
OVERCOMING OBSTACLES

When the Best-laid Plans Fall Short — 158
Show Your True Colors — 159
Getting Tired and Cranky? — 160
Try, Try Again — 162
Unlikely Opportunities — 163
Life in the Trenches — 163

CHAPTER 12 — 169
JUST DO IT

ACKNOWLEDGMENTS — **171**

ABOUT THE AUTHOR — **173**

PREFACE

This book is dedicated to Terry "The Tank" Pritchett, one of my first bosses in sales and the person to whom I owe much of my success and the basis for the ideas in this book.

Terry was the sales manager for a thriving electronics distribution company for which I was a new salesperson. He was a tyrant (or so I thought)! Picture someone who looked like he could play on the front line of an NFL team, who always had a cup of coffee in one hand while holding a cigarette in the other, and whose only speed was full throttle. He demanded we create sales forecasts and plans and complete weekly reports. The sales group met every Monday morning. Each of us who reported to him talked about every opportunity in the categories he had assigned us. He was fanatical about this process and documented our responses on the "war board" in his office. During the week, he constantly demanded answers to questions about our various hot selling opportunities.

After a couple of years, tired of his relentless questioning and all the reporting we were required to do...and weary of being called at my home at 7:00 in the morning to discuss the day's planned activities, I quit.

My next job was with another successful electronics distribution company. They, too, had Monday morning meetings. But their meetings had little structure; instead, they used this valuable time to have coffee and catch up on what had happened over the weekend. They had no forms and no methodologies for detailed tracking and keeping up with what was going on. There was no set plan for success and no formal accountability; every day was a new day. Within two weeks, I got out the forms Terry Pritchett had used and began using them.

What I belatedly realized was that Terry Pritchett was not the tyrant I thought he was, but a sales genius.

I learned that when you track your business daily, weekly, monthly, you can never get too far behind. You automatically will win big, outperform your peers, and make the most money you can make. With this no-fail plan for success, you know EXACTLY where your business stands at all times. You know what tasks need to be managed for each sales opportunity based on its probabilities.

I have used this system in all of my business dealings every day, every month, every year since that time. I believe it is the key to my being able to manage and create more sales and more commissions in my career than I ever thought possible.

This system is the basis of my sales coaching and sales consulting business. I teach all of my clients **how to do this for themselves, step-by-step. With this book, I will show you how to do it, too.**

I will share many client success stories to illustrate what this system can do for a company—and for you.

One of my clients was in the manufacturing business. This privately held business had been in existence for more than 20 years, but their sales had plateaued about three years before I started working with them. When I first met the CEO, he was at a loss as to how the company could get past the plateau and move to the next level. The first thing I noticed was they did not have a sales forecast; In fact they had no sales reporting of any kind. Their sales approach was to simply respond to whoever called on the phone that day. Their system, if you can call it that, was reactive, not proactive.

We immediately began to document on a sales forecast form each customer and any orders in the system. When the CEO saw this information on paper, he was amazed at how much business was already in the pipeline. By the time we had finished identifying their current sales, their outstanding proposals, and their opportunities with other prospects, he was able to see that he had a raft of sales opportunities. We then set out to plan how to systematically address all these opportunities and create a follow-up system. The rest, as they say, is history. In the next six months, the company's sales grew twenty percent.

I find that when clients get back to the fundamentals, things start to happen. Time is spent wisely, clients are serviced properly, and profits go up.

This is not magic. The emphasis is on preparation, good relationships, the power that comes from having a plan, doing what you say you will do, and staying focused on the tasks at hand.

When you are in the midst of a sales action (cold call, needs assessment, presentation/demo or close) and it is hard to remember the solid things that work, you'll be able to refer to this book. Refer to it often—before a call, after a rejection, or just to start the day. I designed it to be a field guide that you carry with you at all times so it's there when you need it—not on a shelf back at the office.

My intent for this book is to help you reach your sales potential faster and to more effectively generate greater revenue for your company and higher commission checks for you.

Awareness paves the path to a more intentional life. Each day, millions of people buy self-help books looking for the "happiness" potion. Each day comes and goes with good intentions of opening those books to learn the secret. And each day passes with more dust settling on the book cover and the person drifting further away from an answer. Why?

We live in a self-help society rife with philosophies and good ideas gone bad. Every day, you can flip on the television for a dose of spirit filling or the expert du jour's advice for fixing your marriage, your kids, or both. I've seen the shows, and I've heard the advice. While there's definitely a place for all of it, what I usually see is a lot of advice without a road map for using it to get the desired result.

That's why I wrote this book. I honor your 168 hours a week and want the time you spend with this "self-help" book to be well spent. I want to give practical, no-nonsense advice that you can put to work right this minute. I want this information to ground you with the basics of successful sales, whether they are new to you or something you are revisiting and reconnecting with. It's as much a place to depart from as a place to come back to.

Are you ready to get back to the fundamentals, hold yourself accountable, and watch sales and profits rise? Then let's go through the Field Guide to Sales system together.

Debbie Mrazek

Debbie Mrazek

INTRODUCTION

Top sales professionals have always been, and continue to be, in demand. Companies can no longer count on an endless supply of experienced professionals waiting to fill the sales function. Additionally, with the cost of replacing these positions, companies increasingly find themselves facing higher recruiting costs, and in some cases, the cost of lost intellectual capital, lost revenue, and lost client relationships can exceed five times a sales professional's salary. Ensuring that sales professionals stay content and challenged is paramount. A sales process that emphasizes the sales professional as a critical component in that process creates a win for the sales professional as well as for the client and employer.

The myriad choices available to customers is staggering. One of the primary ways companies differentiate competition is through human capital—the people who interface with clients. The natural progression of putting people in front of clients is that the relationship falls to the person the client sees most. Management today realizes that while brand loyalty may be lower than it once was, there is still loyalty in the person-to-person relationship. Facilitating a sales process that enables the client to interface with the primary sales contact offers the client an easy way to interact with the company for the long term.

Two primary sales models currently exist: The first is a piecemeal process in which the sales professional fulfills the role of "gatherer" and the client is found, then delivered to the next person in the sales or client service cycle. The challenge with this model is that loyalty to the salesperson is not sufficiently established.

The second model gives management of the entire client relationship to the salesperson. He (or she) handles lead generation, client development, and client care. While good for establishing loyalty, it also can put sales professionals into overload, with too much to do, too much to remember, and too much responsibility. Sales professionals typically have skill sets that support areas of this process and leave other areas untouched and clients mismanaged.

What this book advocates is a third model—one that considers the benefits of a flexible sales process that puts the sales professional in the role of maintaining client-company trust while addressing typical sales weak spots before they can damage the relationship.

This book is not about how a company should manage its sales process but for the salesperson whose company is doing its best to maintain this third model. The book is written for the salesperson who every day, and in every way, is aiming for the sales sweet spot—where the needs of the company are in alignment with the needs of the client, where what the client wants is exactly what the company can deliver, and where client expectations are met.

Creating the sales sweet spot does not require that the sales professional add endless tasks to his or her day. Nor does it require companies to allow sales professionals to go to a non-systemic process where they are required to "do it all" for the client. Instead, it focuses the sales professional on preserving internal as well as external lines of communication.

In short, it helps the salesperson get to that point where asking the right questions at the right time, so the customer will buy.

The intention of the *Field Guide to Sales* is to help you, the sales professional, get back to the fundamentals and focus time, energy, and other resources on the things that matter—for the sales professional, the client and the company.

The question I'm asked most often is this: Why don't I do what I know to do? I don't know.

Like you and many others, I have asked myself that question.

The point—and the practicality this book offers—is it doesn't really matter "why." What matters is what you do when you see you aren't doing what you know.

Through working with my sales clients, I've seen all kinds of reasons why they say "no" to just doing what they know they should do. Maybe they:

* Don't have time.
* Don't believe it really makes a difference.
* Don't think it really will work.
* Don't believe they deserve the great outcome that comes from doing it.
* Don't want to do it.
* Are afraid to start.
* Are in the procrastination habit.
* Have a reason they like to complain about.
* Don't think they are qualified to do it.

All that being said, my experience shows that at some point, people hope and wish that someone will do it for them, wave a magic wand, encourage them, inspire them, and show them the way. Anything to get them off point center—to move, to do, not to be afraid.

Why we don't do what we know to do does not matter, as long as we can figure out how to do it anyway. My experience says the "how to do it" usually involves engaging someone to do it with you—a partner, a coach, a colleague, a friend—someone who believes in you and has no hidden agenda, so you can get rolling and accomplish one thing at a time. Then one day you realize you aren't even conscious that you now do what you know to do. This is the gift of coaching. Changes and results come easily. Without guilt and "shoulds," you simply shift to getting things done, which makes a dramatic difference in getting you where you want to go.

Instead of teaching people how to sell, I want to teach them how to prepare to be there when the customer is ready to buy, so selling becomes easy, comfortable, and fun.

How To Use This Book

The intention of *The Field Guide to Sales* is to help the sales professional get back to the fundamentals and focus time, energy, and other resources on things that matter for the sales professional, the client, and the company.

Whether you're a new salesperson working to get that first client or you've been selling for years, the systematic process is always the same. First, decide what you sell; second, decide whom you'll sell it to; and third, be available to deliver what you say you're going to deliver. When you do that...well, keep doing it so you can repeat it and keep the cycle going on and on and on.

I recommend reading the book through to familiarize yourself with the information, ideas, and exercises. Then go back and focus on the areas where you feel you need the most support today. Choose that section and read it again, study it, go out and practice it, and make notes in the margins. Next time you need support, you'll have my ideas—and yours—to refer to.

The exercises at the end of each chapter are broken down into two parts:

✳ **New Traveler Tips:** for those who are relatively new to sales

✳ **Seasoned Climber Challenges:** for the experienced sales professional

Between the two of us, we can build a great sales success story. Happy selling!

FORECAST: YOUR MAP TO SUCCESS

CHAPTER 1

A savvy traveler, outdoorsman, or adventurer would never dream of departing without a map. For sales professionals, your sales forecast is the single most valuable tool you can pack for the journey.

You Need a Map

Sales is a complex subject, but a simple process.

Statistics show that an average of 80 percent of your sales will come from only 20 percent of your customers. Random sales efforts directed at anyone who *might* buy clearly will result in a lot of wasted time *(yours and* theirs*)*. Top-performing sales professionals don't waste time with the 80 percent who won't buy; they spend their time on those who will buy and buy repeatedly.

Your time is a finite resource, so maximizing it is critical. And that's where a sales forecast comes in. A forecast is an educated guess, based on your past experience, of what your sales will be for a future period of time—over the next quarter or over the next year, say. The forecasting process is a way to get maximum return on your investment of time and energy. Your forecast is a living document that enables you to chart a course—a map that shows you where you are and where you are headed.

Statistics also indicate that 90 percent of all sales come from 10 percent of salespeople. How do they do it? Stellar sales professionals are not micromanaged to perfection by their sales managers; they manage themselves, constantly learning, and always focusing on the activities that deliver the most bang for the buck.

GUIDEPOST 1:
Take the lead role in your own success (because no one else will).

Don't worry about meeting management's minimum expectations. By creating your own goals for success, you'll exceed management's goals for you. No one knows your full potential except you. And with your sales forecast. you will have it all mapped out.

Don't Leave Home Without It

There isn't a profession that doesn't use a plan or forecast as a key element for success. A clear goal, supported by a plan to reach it, is the common denominator in virtually every success story, big or small. To bring home this concept, step outside the sales realm for a moment and consider the following scenarios:

- A lawyer showing up in court without background research or a plan for trying his case
- Elite military forces heading out on a strategic mission without a battle plan
- Doctors in an emergency room randomly treating patients without asking questions or gathering information
- A football team running onto the field without assigned positions or having practiced any plays

Like any other profession, the sales profession has certain techniques and tools that work beautifully when properly implemented. One of these is the sales forecast.

Forecasting requires discipline—just like exercise. You might not like it at first, and it may leave you tired and sore. But, as with exercise, you know you want the expected results. And also as with exercise, you can't simply do it for 30 days and then call it done. Results stop going forward, and even reverse, when you stop.

When you make forecasting a regular part of your sales process, you'll soon experience that the benefits are real—and a whole lot more rewarding than selling without a plan or practice.

Any great sales forecast will grow to include more than numbers. It will illustrate a sales cycle: prospecting, exploring needs, exploring options, presenting a solution, closing, negotiating the contract, servicing the account, and responding to problems and opportunities.

Then, the cycle begins again.

You Don't Have Time NOT to Forecast

I can already hear your objections:

* If I stop to prepare a forecast, I'll lose time.
* I've been a salesperson for 10 years, and I do just fine without a forecast.
* A forecast is just something the sales manager wants from you for the sole purpose of covering himself.
* A sales forecast is just politics. It never helps you, but it could be used as a justification for firing you.
* A forecast is like predicting the future. What is the point of doing something that you know will never be 100 percent accurate?
* I'm a relationship person, and I should be out in the field selling. Let the number crunchers in accounting do the forecasting while I go out and create some revenue.

Great points, but if these are your views on forecasting, you are selling short the most valuable tool in your sales arsenal.

PROOF POSITIVE

One company I worked with had been trying to get over a plateau to reach to a new revenue goal for years. By training each sales professional to use a forecast, this company grew their business 20 percent within six months and ended the year meeting their goal. The following year, they grew their business by another 20 percent.

Welcome to The Trailhead

Before you can create a forecast, you need a strong understanding of the **who, what, and why** of sales for you and your company. This information drives the numbers you will fuel with your potential.

Who?

Who is your ideal client? Is it an individual, an organization, or a company? And if you sell business-to-business, what type of company? Is it a large public company or a small private company? A company with $10 million in revenue and thirty employees? Or a Fortune 500 company with 30,000 employees?

Will you draw your clients from a specific industry? If so, focus on where your customers are in that industry. Use the Web to look for data on your client profile in that industry. I'll talk about some specific resources in the next section.

What?

Do you know what you're selling? Newsflash: the majority of salespeople don't have a clue.

Does McDonald's sell hamburgers? I would argue that McDonald's sells consistency and efficiency. In the same vein, consider these well-known companies and what they actually sell:

* Kodak sells memories.
* Revlon sells the promise of youth and beauty.
* Marlboro sells rugged sophistication.
* Six Flags sells excitement.

Can you solve your customer's problem or fill a need in the same way these companies do? Yes. It's all a matter of looking at the product or service you represent through the eyes of the buyer. What will he or she value enough to buy from you? Hint: It's never the actual product or service. As shown above, it's what they represent.

And from a practical, logistical standpoint, do you know what you sell?

Can your company deliver? Are resources in place to meet the customer's need? Being certain in your answers to these questions makes selling much easier, eliminates doubt and worry for the customer, and makes you successful in the end.

Why?

What is your sales goal? When I ask salespeople that question, they say something like, "Well Deb, I want to do $2 million dollars this year." I follow up with "Would that be $2 million by selling $1 million to two customers or to twenty customers who each buy $100,000?" Clearly, that makes for two very different plans of attack.

Be able to answer that question like you mean business, not as a wishful thinker.

Building Your Forecast, Step-by-Step

To create your forecast, you'll need a piece of grid paper or a spreadsheet on your computer.

The best place to begin is with a known entity: your existing customers.

Existing Customers

1. In the left-hand column, list your customers by company name.

2. Label the next twelve columns by month of the year, starting with the current month.

3. For each month put in the sales dollar amount the customer will spend with you and your company.

4. In the last column you will have the total for that customer.

Outstanding Proposals: Follow the same exercise for outstanding proposals you have submitted to potential clients. A proposal is a document that details what you plan to do together with a dollar amount attached. Put that number in the column that corresponds with when you think the business will begin.

Hard Leads: A hard lead is a scenario in which, with the client, you have defined an opportunity or a piece of business. Another way to define a hard lead is as an identified opportunity, which typically happens after two to three conversations. Quantify the opportunity and record it in the month you think it would begin.

Prospects: A prospect is someone you know and who knows you. You have obtained their information and gathered pertinent facts about their company; perhaps you've had a productive conversation that left you with a good sense of how you might do business together. This conversation has allowed you to better quantify what the opportunity might be and you record your projection.

Suspects: Suspects are possible clients you have found through research or stumbled across in your travels. This client either sounds like a fit based on what you know or has strong similarities to a company you already do business with. Suspects don't know you, and you don't know them—until you make contact and determine if the suspect is a prospect or a dead end. Quantify a potential opportunity with a suspect by your experience with similar clients you already do business with.

Timing is Everything

Each month, you will create a new forecast for the last month on the sheet. The first column each month will always be the next month; hence, the term "rolling forecast."

You do not have to be great to get started, but you do have to get started to be great. Your job today is to just get started. This forecast gives you a place to keep a daily record. When you have identified all of your opportunities, from suspect to customer, and you have quantified each of those opportunities, you will have a subtotal for each category and a grand total at the bottom.

CONTACT	MONTH 1	2	3	12	TOTAL
SUSPECT					
SUBTOTAL					
PROSPECT					
SUBTOTAL					
HARD LEAD					
SUBTOTAL					
OUTSTANDING PROPOSALS					
SUBTOTAL					
CUSTOMERS					
SUBTOTAL					
GRAND TOTAL					

THE FIELD GUIDE TO SALES

Your sales forecast is not a document you create and then file away; it's a tool you're going to use every day to see how you are progressing with your sales plan. Instead of waiting for 90 days or an annual review to see how someone else thinks you are doing, *you will know at a glance how well you are doing at any point in time.*

PROOF POSITIVE

At one company I worked for, salespeople routinely prepared their next year's forecast between Christmas and New Year's—a time we were uninterested in doing a forecast, or much else, for that matter. So the tendency was to plug in a number that sounded good but that had no basis in reality.

Guess what happened every year? Management tried to manage to that forecast, but at the end of the next year, the projected results never materialized. In fact, the projections had no relation to the results they were projecting, let alone results that correlated to the forecast.

If you want to add a level of sophistication to your forecast, add a column for probabilities. For instance you might feel there is a 70 percent probability that a certain hard lead will move forward to the proposal stage. Referring to the probabilities column will not only help you prioritize how you manage your time, but in retrospect, it will give you a gauge of how attuned you are to each deal.

Prioritize with Success in Mind

Your existing customers are always your top priority; then come proposals, followed by hard leads, prospects, and finally, suspects.
  Prioritizing based on your sales forecast is something you can do each day with your PDA, computer, or other planning system. It's up to

you how you use it and whether you use an electronic or paper system. What's important is to use it.

There is no excuse not to have your sales forecast with you at all times so you can update it on the fly. Your forecast is your most important document, so it must *always* be up-to-date.

Put Your Forecast to Work

Do you see yourself below?

* This forecast is working really well. I've already got three customers out of it and have ten proposals in the works. I've qualified forty prospects. My pipeline is full!

* Some of my hard leads went cold, and my current customers aren't bringing in what I projected. I need to add more new suspects.

In either situation, knowing is better than not knowing. Unless the plan exists in a format that's easily read and managed, *you know and I know that you won't use it more than once.*

GUIDEPOST 2:
Forecast for accountability.

Only when you update your forecast on a daily and weekly basis does it become a tool to help you grow your business in a meaningful, intentional way. Not only that, it helps you communicate within your company what resources and preparations are going to be needed to handle business that is coming.

Using a dynamic tool like the sales forecast can have an immediate and dramatic impact on your business.

Use the Forecast as an Early Warning System

After you have been using your forecast for three months, look back on the last 90 days. What do you need to adjust? Do you need to add suspects, or do you have too many? Have you been lax in following up on proposals? What adjustment will have the greatest impact on your bottom line?

GUIDEPOST 3:
Respond to the difference between actual sales versus forecast sales.

FIELD STUDIES

1. Log on to www.naics.com to find the North American Industrial Classification System six-digit code that best describes your ideal client. Start with simple keywords and read the specific definitions until you find the code(s) that best describe that type of company. Then go to the www.census.gov U.S. Census website and type in that NAICS code to find detailed information on that industry.

2. Use www.google.com to look up key words related to that industry.

3. Find the industry trade association by using www.businessfinance.com/tradeassociations.htm

4. Through the trade association, find out which companies are members.

5. Research individual companies through Google searches of their Websites and by using resources such as ReferenceUSA (usually available at public or university libraries) or Hoover's Online (www.hoovers.com) or Dun & Bradstreet (www.dnb.com).

An ideal client will be of a specific size, in a specific industry, financially sound and growing, and perhaps located in a specific geographical area.

Your job is to create a list of these ideal prospects that will help define your sales pipeline: suspects, prospects, hard leads, outstanding proposals, and customers.

NEW TRAVELER TIPS

If you have never created a forecast, the best way to do it is to start with the customers.

* Who are your customers, and how are their dollars planned for the year?
* Is there a seasonal aspect to your business that your planning has to follow?
* Do you take orders from them monthly or on a different time frame?

Next, look at outstanding proposals:

* What proposals do you have outstanding?
* What is the value of those proposals?

Then, work your way through your hard leads, prospects, and suspects. Don't worry about capturing them all—you will be continually adding to your database.

 **SEASONED CLIMBER CHALLENGE**

Consider how your business and your forecasting would be affected if:

* You lost your biggest customer.
* A supplier problem forced your company to stop delivering your best-selling product.
* Your long-time contact at your biggest customer left for a new job.
* A competitor cuts prices or develops a new faster/better/cheaper product.

ASKDEB

Q: I am an Executive Technical Recruiter with a focus on management through executive level positions within technology companies. I enjoy working with small- to medium-sized companies. Even though I call people all day, I am paralyzed when it comes to the business development calls I need to make in order to get new clients.

I probably need three small companies and a couple mid-sized companies to keep me busy all year. Rationally, I know it will take somewhere between 100 and 200 cold calls. But I freeze up and just stare at the phone!

How can I get over my fear of cold calling?

A: *People are usually afraid of selling for one of two reasons. One, they are afraid of someone rejecting what they have to offer. The other is people are often not completely convinced that what they are offering is that great, so they're afraid to sell it because someone else won't really like it or need it.*

If you believe in what you have to offer, hold your head high, put your shoulders back, and get on the phone and start calling people and making appointments with the EXPECTATION that they will ABSOLUTELY want to see you and learn how you can help them!

If you are putting out fear, you are probably getting something less than great in return—like, no new business. If you put out confidence and belief in yourself, the world will reward you with the same!

Want more help on your journey?

See www.TheFieldGuideToSales.com for the Forecast: Your Map to Success Workbook

YOUR ITINERARY

CHAPTER 2

Once you know where you are headed—thanks to your sales forecast—you'll have a feel for what needs to happen along the way and what you need to do when you arrive at your destination. As a sales professional, how you assign your time—before, during, and after the sale—is vital to your success.

How Will You Spend the Next 168 Hours?

Time management is about choices. Actions always speak louder than words. Where you are spending your time will give big clues about your life and work choices.

Many people think time management is about cleaning up your desk, putting things in neat piles, and then working on them, tackling the most urgent item first. In my opinion, many of us spend way too much time cleaning up the mess and reacting to everything that crosses our path. Busy is not the same as productive.

Don't spend any more time than you have to with things; spend your time with people.

PROOF POSITIVE

A Watson-Wyatt Worldwide study concluded that the most successful salespeople spend 40 percent more time with their best potential customers and three to four additional hours above the average each week performing high-value sales activities, such as identifying customer needs and forecasting.

These very same sales people spend 30 percent less time on administrative duties.

Find out where you are spending the precious commodity of time by monitoring how you use yours for the next week. Keep an hour-by-hour log for seven days. Determine the percentage of time you spend in each of these areas:

* Sleeping
* Personal time (with family, eating, socializing, recreation, hobbies, etc.)
* Commuting

* On the phone with customers
* Face-to-face with customers
* Working on proposals or preparing for customer meetings
* Researching and listing suspect and prospects
* Working on your forecast
* Administration

If there are other categories that represent more than a few hours each week, list them as well.

You will have to determine how happy you are with the percentage of time you spend sleeping, commuting to work, spending time with family and friends, etc. Those are choices for you to make.

When it comes to work time, you also have some options. For example, could you find two more hours for selling each week? If you could spend two more hours a week selling, how much more could you sell?

PROOF POSITIVE

When I monitor my time (which I continue to do periodically, and so should you) I found extra hours in a variety of places, none of which cramped my style, and most of which left me happy with enough of the "wasted time" we all need:

- During my kids' sports practices (but never during games)!

- While waiting for appointments and between appointments. (This was the biggest time sucker for me; instead of heading for a coffee shop where I could review notes or work through paperwork, I gravitated to the nearest mall, which cost me in more ways than one.)

- Not watching mind-numbing reruns of TV shows I don't like anyway.

- Getting out of bed when I wake up instead of lying in bed waiting for the alarm clock to ring.

If you are like the typical salesperson, you spend a lot of time commuting and a lot of time in administration, but relatively little time with customers and prospects or actively planning your time with them. Turning that around is one of the highest-impact things you can do to increase your speed down the road to success.

Here is a list of the typical sales responsibilities:

- Closing sales
- Meeting with current clients
- Meeting with a hard lead
- Writing proposals
- Meeting with prospects
- Attending networking events
- Researching and developing suspects
- Making phone calls to set appointments
- Asking for referrals
- Servicing customers
- Attending Internal meetings
- Completing Administrative paperwork

Out of the working hours you tracked before, can you quantify the percentage of time you spend on each of these activities?

How Much Time Do You Really Have?

You don't sell 365 days a year. In fact, you may be surprised to find that if you count weekends, vacations, company meetings, training seminars, illness, or personal issues, you may have only 100 net selling days a year. Considering how many customers and prospects you have, you can calculate how many calls you need to be making to achieve your goals.

Learning to manage your time in sales by being prepared is like with, or in every other profession. It is critical, dynamic, and produces predictable, consistent results. There is no one system that works for everybody. You'll need to try different things to find what works for you.

Changing Your View of Time

Start changing your view of time by acknowledging that you actually enjoy wasting it. Time management is about choices, not all the time, but some of the time. It feels good to get something done, even if that something is of little consequence. But filling too much time with activities that have little influence on productivity or results eats away at your success.

It's amazing how much time goes by talking about the game, hearing the office gossip, reading the paper (or email), and running errands. None of these things are bad, but they rank high on the list of time wasters.

If you want to get serious about improving your sales career, you must get serious about how you spend your time. Evaluate each task you do by asking yourself the following:

* Could I delegate this task to someone else?
* Will this task result in an increase in business or in my potential to do business with this company?
* Is this just part of the routine I've fallen into, or is it something I really want to do?
* Am I spending time with this because I like the client and want to help, or is it because this is a high-value way to spend my time?

GUIDEPOST 4:
Do the things first that most directly relate to your goals.

PROOF POSITIVE

A Fortune 500 company sales VP didn't think his sales team's performance was on a par with their potential, so he hired me to coach his team on their time management.

I could feel the chill when I walked into the room to meet with the four sales executives. Sue, arms folded across her chest and her forehead knit in a frown, seemed particularly unhappy to see me. I knew this wasn't going to be easy, but I had faith in the process

I emphasized to them that this training was an investment the company was making in them, not only as professionals but as people. I explained how my system would work and gave them their "homework." The body language around the conference table remained hostile.

Sue was not happy about the assignment and told me as much. I listened to her and told her to just give it the time she had to spare. With little more than a huff, she left the room, and I left the meeting less than confident about the results I hoped each person would see.

I was back at the company a week later to follow up on the homework assignment. As I pulled up, I saw Sue, clearly upset, standing beside her car, waiting for me. I gathered my briefcase, and my muster, and approached her.

"I can't believe this!" she exclaimed before I could say a word. "I can't believe I spend 14 hours a week in traffic. No wonder I'm a wreck by the time I get home!"

Tears welled in her eyes. "Do you really think you can help me?" she pleaded. I was sure I could help her now that she was beginning to understand the problem.

Once we started looking at her time map, we discovered many areas where she could pull "double duty" without compromising the task at hand. For instance, she could work different hours and visit customers on her way in to the office to drastically reduce time on the road. And in her remaining travel time, she could listen to sales training tapes.

We found her biggest use of time was responding to everyone else's needs, leaving her no time to get to the things that were critical to her success. We immediately made her unavailable for meetings on Friday and put that time to use for planning.

Sue seemed happy with the action plan we developed. I talked to her a few weeks later to see how the plan was working and was delighted to hear that she had made noticeable improvements not only in her drive time, but in other areas as well—including her work. By balancing her time schedule, she was able to fit everything into her life that was important.

Customers Have Expectations About How You Should Spend Your Time

Big surprise: Customers think you should spend the majority of your time with them. Based on a study by J.D. Power and Associates on wireless retail sales satisfaction, this might not be such a bad idea.

PROOF POSITIVE

The average wait time before customers are greeted after they first enter a wireless retail store is approximately five minutes. The study noted that overall satisfaction with the sales experience declines considerably if the wait time exceeds 30 seconds.

The study found that customers who are approached within 30 seconds of entering the store provide a satisfaction score that is more than 10 percent higher than customers who are not greeted as quickly. Customers who were not greeted in a timely manner said they were 32 percent less likely to visit that store again.

As you might expect, as the amount of time spent during the wireless retail sales transaction increases, customer satisfaction decreases. The average wireless retail sales transaction takes nearly one hour to complete from the time the customer enters the store to the time the paperwork is finished and the product is received.

Not a single customer satisfaction statistic talks about how much time the salesperson spends commuting, improving his sales skills or reporting to management. Customers want focused attention, filled with information that will help them solve a problem.

Time has become a precious commodity. Fewer people expect or have time for long lunches, golf excursions, and the like. They just want answers.

Customers today really are more demanding. Why? Because they have easy access, more information, and more alternatives than in the past. If you can't help them make money or save money, they are on to the next option. It's your job to capture and keep their attention.

The Internet allows you to know more about your customers than ever before. It also allows them to do their homework before they buy.

Your customers may know more about your products and your competition than you do!

The time for show and tell about your product has been all but replaced by the time to explain how it will integrate with an existing system. The expectation is that the time you will spend with your customer is high-quality, productive time for both of you.

GUIDEPOST 5:
High-value time spent with customers and on high-value sales activities positions you for high-value success.

The Shortest Distance Between Two Points

Have you ever considered that three minutes of planning might be worth thousands of dollars in return? As experienced salespeople will tell you, the most effective way to move a sale from point A to point B is by being prepared and being present.

* How do your sales calls go?
* Do you plan for them, or do they routinely take longer than you expect?
* Do you accomplish what you intended?
* Are you making calls just to see which ones stick, or have you identified a demonstrated need for your product or service?

If a customer or prospect has given you a valuable piece of their precious day, don't waste it by being unprepared.

More than sales training, or memorizing your company's message, or demonstrating the product, the way to use sales call time most wisely is to think about and plan for it.

Lifestyle = "Salestyle"

Now, let's step back and look at the big picture of time. From the moment you drew your first breath, you have been spending your "life time." Your choices reflect what is important to you at every moment—regardless of whether you are conscious of it. In short, actions speak louder than words.

What do your actions say about you? What is most important to you right now? Do you know? Do you decide how you will live your life, or is your life a series of moments that simply happen?

How we spend time molds our character, documents our existence and, ultimately, shapes our destiny.

Just think about it. You start each week with a blank slate of time at your command. Each week, you have 168 hours of life time to use as you see fit. Regardless of our status in society, our bank account, or education level, we all begin and end each week with the same 168 hours.

Time is as unforgiving as it is comfortably stable. We cannot barter it, steal it, negotiate it, trade it, give it, take it, or change it. It is a gift for each of us to spend as we will. The choice we must make is whether our time will be spent intentionally or haphazardly.

GUIDEPOST 6:

Time management is life management.

FIELD STUDIES

Review or research the following before your next sales call with an important client:

* How did they get from suspect to client? What is the recent history — good and bad?
* Who is the decision-maker?
* Is the client public or private? Financially sound?
* What is the expected lifetime value of the client?
* Who in your existing circle of influence may know this client and give you more information on their status and needs?

Plan your sales call to meet one of these objectives:

* Close the sale.
* Learn about a new need you might be able to fill that would increase the business they do with you.
* Get a qualified referral to the person who can move the decision to the next step.
* Gather additional information for a proposal you are preparing.

NEW TRAVELER TIPS

Looking at how you actually spent your 168 hours this past week, create a time forecast for next week. Proactively decide how much time you will spend with family, friends, and recreation, and how much time you will spend working.

With that working time, decide how much time you will spend on administrative activities versus with clients. Then keep another log of your actual time to judge how much progress you've made.

SEASONED CLIMBER CHALLENGE

If you found out one of your major clients was going through troubled times, how would it change your next sales call? Would you use your time differently? If so, how?

If your sales manager came to you and said that a corporate division might close unless sales improved dramatically in the next 90 days, what would you do?

If your company discontinued one of the products purchased most often by your top clients, what would you do?

ASK DEB

Q: When I have sales appointments with prospects I always call the day before to confirm. I'm not sure whether this is a good strategy since I find that this gives people the opportunity to cancel at the last minute. The downside of not calling to confirm is I have had a few "no-shows," which is a waste of my time. What should I do?

A: *If people are canceling or not showing up at the appointment, it generally means you have not qualified them properly up front. If we do our jobs right, they are looking forward to seeing us because they know we are there to help them solve a significant problem.*

Prospects who don't show up communicate unstated objections, such as:

- *I'm not sure how you can help me.*
- *I'm not sure I need your help.*
- *I don't know you that well.*
- *I'm not sure you understand my needs.*

Take this as an opportunity to rethink your prospect qualification process, and you will find prospects making time for you.

Want more help on your journey?

See www.TheFieldGuideToSales.com for the Your Itinerary Workbook.

YOUR ITINERARY

YOUR BACKPACK & PROVISIONS

CHAPTER 3

You've got your map. You've got your itinerary. Now all you need is a big enough supply of information to fill your pack and sustain you through the sales cycles ahead. Information will drive your every action and interaction. This information will relate to both tangible and intangible facets of you, your customer, your company, your co-workers, and the industry.

The key to great selling is helping people prepare to buy. Doing so takes some preparation on your part to determine where you can make a contribution, sharing who you are and what you do, and making it easy to do business with you.

Get Your Bearings

Every sale has a cycle, and while this cycle has a beginning, it doesn't end; rather, it repeats, with new details and objectives, and runs for the duration of the salesperson/client relationship.

Every client entered the cycle as a suspect or prospect. As an individual or company enters your sales cycle, you begin an interactive process to discover their needs and the options for filling those needs. With the proposal, you present a solution. When you finally decide on all the parts to that solution, you close the sale with a contract or product delivery and payment.

After the initial sale is complete, there is ongoing service to respond to problems and build new opportunities.

How you prepare for any sales call depends on where the client is in this cycle. It's up to you to stay on top of where each deal with each customer stands in the cycle. Think of it as your compass for moving forward.

Become Familiar with Your Surroundings

Begin by getting to know the customer. How can you prepare to present a great solution unless you know the customer, his business, and most important, his problems and concerns? Use your sales binoculars to take in the surroundings so you can make a meaningful contribution.

Can you help make the customer's business more profitable and effective? Do you have enough information and data to present options that will increase his revenue, cut his costs, or save him time?

Get to Know the Locals

Make no mistake—when I say the customer (or prospect), I mean the decision-maker; the buyer for what you sell. If you aren't talking with the decision-maker, you are also wasting both the customer's time and yours.

One of the biggest advantages you can have is a champion in the company—someone other than the decision-maker with whom you've developed a relationship, who would like to do business with you, and who is in a position to help make that happen.

Get out your field notebook and butterfly net! Your champion can be a tremendous resource as you gather information about revenue-generating cost-reduction opportunities that will determine your solution. You are looking for the person who will have the answers to these questions about the prospective customer:

* How long have you been in business?
* What is the nature of your product?
* Who makes up your client base?
* What is your current sales value?
* Did you make your numbers last year?
* Have you set your numbers for this year?
* Do you sell your product globally? Or only in the United States?
* Do you have offices all over the world?
* Do you partner with other have companies to make your product?
* Is your product a stand-alone product?
* Are you profitable?
* Are you as profitable as you want to be?
* What is your strategy?
* How do you market your product or service?

YOUR BACKPACK & PROVISIONS   49

* What is your target audience?
* Who are some of the major customers you are targeting?
* What is the value or the benefit of your product or service?
* Who are your competitors?
* How does your product or service differ from your competitors'?
* Who handles your sales and marketing now, and how is that working?
* Does anyone on your management team have experience in the new area you are trying to go after, or are you starting from scratch?
* Are you going to be hiring extra people?
* Are there technology limitations in your company?
* How would you define success for this venture?

When you know these things about your clients, you have the source for an amazing transformation in your business. In the course of analyzing this information, you are likely to uncover the unexpected. This is your opportunity to determine if the prospect is really a good customer for you and, if so, how you can most profitably do business together.

GUIDEPOST 7:
Assess what the customer really thinks about the buying experience and map your course accordingly.

Double-check Your Supply List

Make sure your "backpack" has plenty of knowledge and enthusiasm. People buy from you because of passion and persuasion, not because of pretty sales brochures, so when you think of preparing your material, plan printed material as something to leave behind, not something to focus on during the meeting.

The first step in preparation is get out of your head and into your customer's shoes. Are you ready to sell benefits and not features? Do you have a system for asking the right questions and giving the most valuable information?

Do You Hear an Echo?

Along with knowledge and enthusiasm, make sure you bring along a positive attitude. When was the last time a customer asked, "What do we need to do to get started?" For great salespeople, that's a regular occurrence because they get back what they put out there: a great attitude and great energy.

How do you make your clients feel when they buy from you? Start finding clues in what they say to you:

- "This has been the best experience. Thank you so much for making a difference in our business."

- "You know, this was really painful, and I do not want to do it like this again."

- "I thought you were great, but I couldn't believe how rude your customer service people were with me."

- "You told me I would be able to get my order in three days, and it took seven. I liked you personally, but I couldn't consider working with a company I can't count on to do what it said it would."

- "We were able to improve our manufacturing output because we had no downtime thanks to how well your product worked."

- "We improved profitability last quarter because your service helped us to be more efficient."

If you don't hear the good stuff as often as you'd like, solve the problem. Know your product, know what the company is realistically able to deliver, help the other people at your company know what they need to do to satisfy your customers. Leave nothing to chance. It is your responsibility to manage expectations.

A Word about Attitude

Don't you love it when you can't wait to do something? It's a much different feeling than "having to" or "supposing you should." Or how about this feeling:

> *"Well, I have to do this. The same old same old dance. Small talk followed by the stupid questions before I can start talking and get them to do my deal."*

We don't perform the "shoulds" or "have to's" consistently or with much exuberance, but we do "want to's" all the time and with no reminders. So how can you create "want to" in place of "have to"?

Look for the place in your sales process where "should" and "want to" collide. It's there, but it may be hard to see if you're feeling defeated. It's no secret that getting the sale is intoxicating for most sales professionals. Many will tell you it is more rewarding than getting the commission check. So if you "want to" get the sale so badly, turn the "shoulds" into exciting steps toward making that happen.

You know you want to get paid, and the way that you get paid is by selling something. So shouldn't you want to invest the time and energy it will take to set up the deal properly in the first place? That's what produces the winning attitude.

GUIDEPOST 8:
*Prepare not only your material,
but also your attitude.*

Sore Muscles

Did you pack the liniment? Salespeople spend much of their time thinking about their weaknesses and how they can improve. The result is they often spend an inordinate amount of time focused on what they do poorly instead of on what they do well.

As we grow up, we are taught to learn from our mistakes. While I agree with this to a point, I believe we need to shift our thinking to learn from our successes as well.

What are your top five strengths as a salesperson? If you could shore up your strengths, would you be able to sidestep your weaknesses and make them less relevant?

If your strength in sales is closing deals, then you should have others around you who excel at identifying opportunities, setting appointments, creating presentations. You don't have to do everything well.

PROOF POSITIVE

For year, I sold technology products. I always felt as though I should go back to school and get a degree in engineering so I could talk more technically about what I was selling. In the process, I dismissed the fact that my strengths were listening and connecting people.

I also missed the fact that my customers never expected me to be able to "design" the semiconductors and printed circuit boards I was selling. What they needed was for me to listen to them, understand what they said, and connect them to the solutions they needed.

Study your strengths and focus on how you can make them stronger to grow your sales. Let your weaknesses be someone else's strength and partner with them for your combined success in selling.

If you're going to be a professional salesperson, you've got to continue to study all your life. Commit to investing in your education and growing your knowledge.

Until recently, sales was not even taught in universities. You could major in marketing, but not in sales. It was up to salespeople to learn whatever they could, however they could, on the fly.

One Foot in Front of the Other

I dislike the word practice. Instead, I prefer performance as a sure-fire method to strengthen your strengths. The more often you perform, the more comfortable it becomes, and the more enjoyable it is to do.

Are you approaching each new sales call the same way? Have you developed a system that works? Is it repeatable? Is it comfortable for you?

Or is every sale a whole new experience?

Similarly, how prepared are you when you see an existing client? Do you approach the existing client as casually as you would a next-door neighbor, or do you see an existing client with a prepared plan? What about the next sale? How will you be involved in the next project he is thinking of? How are you going to be part of the decision-making process of thinking about what product he is going to be using next?

Without fail, each meeting, each encounter should have both an agenda and a goal for that interaction. And each one should sharpen your delivery and pitch.

If you were thinking of lifetime relationships, would that change the way your agenda reads today for your interaction with that client? Would you be less assertive or aggressive about getting the order today, putting pressure on the client, intentionally making him uncomfortable if he doesn't buy?

Do you think you've failed if you don't make the sale, even if you've taken a positive step in the process?

Meeting new people, having meaningful conversations about things you both believe in, and helping them take their businesses to the next level... who wouldn't want to do that?

If you were prepared, had an agenda, and took the next steps to a sale, and you and your client had an enjoyable, productive experience, *congratulate yourself.*

GUIDEPOST 9:
Never lose sight of the lifetime value of the client.

Why this message is so important is simple: People love to buy things, but they hate to be sold. Salespeople have the distinction of ranking right up there with dentists and the IRS in terms of popularity.

Being sold is unpleasant. As the seller, it's your job to help customers discover the characteristics that make your product or service unique and gratifying to purchase.

FIELD STUDIES

Successful salespeople are:

* Committed.
* Consistent.
* Curious.
* Contagious.
* Concise.
* Caring.

How do you rate yourself in each of these areas on a scale of 1-10?

NEW TRAVELER TIPS

Start with the basics with big pay-offs:

* Create a lead-tracking and follow-up system that works for you. Make sure it has all relevant information and a tickler for next steps.

* Create an account profile for your top three customers and your top three hard leads. What is your strategy to get or keep these accounts? What is your annual revenue goal for each account? What is the time frame to the first or next sale?

With these two tools in your pack, you will be more ready than ever to maximize your sales opportunities.

SEASONED CLIMBER CHALLENGE

An expert is always prepared, so think about these:

* How would you change your sales approach if your company decided to change its emphasis from new sales to more profitable sales with current clients and changed your compensation accordingly?

* What strategies get you reenergized and engaged when you are in a sales slump?

* What would you do if your greatest champion at your most significant client told you he was leaving to take a job at a competitive company?

ASK DEB

Q: Are the best sales candidates interested in the lower base and higher incentive form of compensation?

A: *I think the best salespeople are those who have a lower base and a higher incentive. The catch is, what is a lower base? In some businesses, a low base would be $30K plus an incentive program, whereas in others, it would be a low base of $120K plus an incentive program.*

My rule of thumb is to allow great salespeople to be great salespeople by alleviating them from worrying about where their next meal will come from or whether can they keep the lights on at their house.

Each of us is different, so work with your salesperson to structure a base he can comfortably live on. Invest this effort up front, and your salesperson won't expend valuable time and energy — time and energy they should be using to grow sales — on worrying about their personal finances.

Structuring the right base gives your salesperson the security of knowing his basic needs are taken care of but that he cannot be complacent in performance because he or she wants the incentive part of the package to do many other things like travel, send kids to college, buy a bigger house, save for retirement, etc…

Salespeople perform best when they are allowed to do what they do best and are acknowledged for it with appreciation and compensation.

I do not believe in compensation caps. A cap is poison to a truly great salesperson. If he is capable of selling more, why discourage him for doing so? It's counter-intuitive. If your company is making money on the transaction, continue to find a way to share that success with your salesperson.

Conversely, I am puzzled as to why companies don't shape their compensation plans to pay less to salespeople who sell a little versus a lot. For example, a company will pay five percent for the first million dollars someone sells but only three percent if he sells $5 million. Great salespeople are generally motivated by both money and reward. If they can make more by selling more versus selling less and making a higher percentage that equates to less money, why would they not aim for the $5 million that would serve them better—and serve the employer better as well? And logical as this is, I have yet to find a company structured this way.

Want more help on your journey?

See www.TheFieldGuideToSales.com for the Your Backpack & Provisions Workbook

THE LANDSCAPE

CHAPTER 4

As you start hiking down the sales trail, you'll find that one of the most exhilarating and enjoyable parts of this trip is the constantly changing terrain. Taking into account the perspectives of everyone involved in the sales process is an effective step toward the sale.

Expectations are everywhere. You can't escape them, you can't ignore them, but you can use your empathy and understanding of them to your advantage in making a sale work well for all involved.

We all have expectations of each other:

* You have them of your company, the other members of your team, and even your customers.
* Your company is counting on you and has expectations of your performance that may be critical to its long-term success.
* Prospects and customers have expectations of you and your company to do what you say you will.

The sales professional is tasked with managing all sorts of client expectations. To be successful in sales, salespeople must take a proactive role in helping to set expectations, or at least to manage them.

We'll start by exploring the expectations that are easiest to manage: your own.

Your Expectations of Yourself

Successful salespeople are optimists by nature. They may even appear to have an inflated expectation of their performance and success rate. They work with the belief that only good things are going to happen. They are going to get the largest possible orders, and the customer is going to buy everything and continue to buy.

Part of the reason many salespeople don't like to do research is that what they find may put a damper on those expectations. But one of the characteristics that separates the professionals from the amateurs is that professionals are thirsty for information that will help them make the best sale possible under the conditions and variables at hand.

Salespeople like to think that nothing will go wrong during the sales process *even though they know better from experience.* It's this view through rose-colored glasses that gives many people their negative opinion about salespeople across the board.

PROOF POSITIVE

Think of the stereotypical car salesperson who tells you what you want to hear and gives you the impression that you have a deal. But then he leaves you for 20 minutes to get an okay from the sales manager, only to return with the news that he actually can't deliver on the expectation he set.

This happened to me. It left me angry and the salesperson without a sale. Given what I do for a living, I have an extremely low tolerance for such games and poor planning.

Having real knowledge and understanding of the customer, an honest or realistic understanding of the customer's problem, and the service your company can provide allows you to set a realistic expectation of what you can deliver.

Salespeople love the high of the win and are devastated when they lose the deal. Setting realistic expectations of your own performance is one of the kindest things you can do to help yourself. Sometimes that big deal is just not realistic—yet.

Where are the expected roadblocks? What could possibly go wrong? Playing out those scenarios as if everything is going to go perfectly gives you a goal. On the other hand, considering what might go wrong helps you to forecast realistically.

GUIDEPOST 10:

Be positive and realistic about what could happen between now and the sale.

Give yourself a break. In the beginning of the sales relationship, your goal is simply to build trust and rapport. Help the customer build important expectations of you and your company, such as dependability, responsiveness, and integrity.

If you manage to set high expectations and meet them, you've met your initial goals for the relationship. Build relationships, and sales will follow.

Your Expectations of Your Customers

I have good news. From this day forward you no longer have to worry whether or not each person you talk to will buy from you. They won't.

Your job is to get out there and interact with suspects, prospects, and customers to identify the ones who are a fit. These are the ones who will be open to partnering and who comfortably say, "I need what you've got. Let's talk." The relationship will naturally escalate from there.

Relationships are the reason asking open-ended questions is so great for establishing and managing expectations. Much more information flows in a dialogue than when you are working from a checklist of questions, especially when some are too easily answered yes or no. Go for the easy, open conversation.

PROOF POSITIVE

I talk about this in my program, "I Hate Sales and So Should You!"

- Do you want this? Do you want that?
- Do you have this? Do you have that?
- Do you see a need for this? Or that?

We all hate to be approached to buy in this way. Can salespeople really be surprised when the deal goes nowhere?

Your expectation should be that this is not a one-time sale—you are going to have a relationship with this customer. Certainly, some sales are, by nature, one-time, but even those should carry the expectation of a lasting professional relationship. No matter how much or how little a customer buys, part of the deal should always be that human connection that goes beyond the sale. That human connection is what will move the customer to refer you to others.

Your Expectations of Your Company and Coworkers

Imagine that it's taken you a year to get a piece of business. You got the signature, you got the check, but then your company doesn't deliver. Where does that leave you?

Customers trust and believe in you. They have a certain impression and expectation of you that they believe translates back to the company you represent. They expect the company to behave like you behave. Sadly, this isn't always the case.

It's demoralizing to a salesperson when he does a beautiful job with the customer—getting to know him, teaching him, showing him what the company can do for him, preparing the proposal, closing the deal—only to have his company fail to follow through. The customer is disappointed and does not want to hear excuses about whose fault it is or isn't. Blame is not the issue.

The salesperson often bears the brunt of the customer's frustration—and rightfully so. The salesperson represents the company, and the customer has the right to expect that everything will go as planned and that the issue will be taken care of quickly and accordingly.

Consider this: A really great salesperson, even if the company has dropped the ball, can manage customer expectations, realigning them to save the situation and, most important, the relationship (*and sometimes the order*).

PROOF POSITIVE

A printing company salesperson I know told me a great story of how he turned a bad situation into a plum account.

He had just landed one of the largest accounts of his career, for a local school district. It would involve regularly paced projects as well as special one-time projects throughout the year. He worked directly with the deputy superintendent who assigned the projects.

Not long into the contract, the deputy superintendent needed materials for a trade show he would be traveling to. Most everything got finished but owing to an internal communication issue, important handouts and business cards would not be printed on time.

Thinking on his feet, the salesperson contacted a printer in the city where the trade show was being be held and electronically relayed the document files for printing. He then contacted the customer, explained the situation, and offered free packing and shipping of all conference materials.

Everything was waiting in the customer's hotel room upon his arrival.

A skilled salesperson can adjust for many company imperfections by how he handles a customer, the relationship he builds with him, and the communications they establish.

Terrific salespeople can often seamlessly turn a difficult situation into a "Wow!" situation. A "Wow!" situation is one in which something was so poorly handled that the customer plans to take this and all future business elsewhere, but the heroic salesperson acts quickly to solve the problem, resulting in the customer's continuing to do business with the company and even referring others. These can be a salesperson's greatest moments.

Having said all of that, what can you expect of your company and your co-workers when you are making a sale? It's a matter of people working together and understanding shared objectives.

PROOF POSITIVE

One company I worked with had a long-festering communication breakdown between the sales force and the accounting department. There seemed always to be an underlying tone of animosity that everyone acknowledged but no one addressed.

In came a new CEO who insisted on more open flow of communication between departments. She was a proponent of company-wide meetings to review goals, objectives, plans, and concerns, always soliciting input from employees—much different than the dictatorial style we had all grown used to.

It turned out that the animosity was based on the accountants' feeling rebuffed. The company had to meet quarterly loan covenants that could have been helped by additional revenue, and time-sensitive reporting tasks that relied on input from sales that was always slow to arrive. This unresponsiveness on the part of the sales department left the accounting people feeling ignored and undervalued.

But the sales department had no inkling of the problem, so it's no wonder no one stepped up to the plate in support of the accounting department.

A few additional calls by the sales force with a special discount could have brought in an earlier order to bring in extra revenue by quarter's end—a reminder during busy times that reporting was needed and that it would have solved the information flow problem.

If your production department isn't aware that you have a big project in the pipeline they could be ramping up for, who is really to blame when your customer's deadline falls by the wayside?

Your co-workers aren't mind readers. Tell them what you need, and understand what they need. In a sense, this oils the cogs in the bigger system that supports the success of your sale. If everyone understands the what and why of everyone else's function in the system, things are likely to run much more smoothly and with much more goodwill.

What Customers and Prospects Expect of You.

"You didn't keep your promise."

That's the sound of a customer or prospect telling you that you've lost some credibility and diminished the trust in your relationship.

From your first conversation with the prospect, you leave clues about yourself and your company that he takes into consideration when deciding to do business with you.

* Were you on time?

* Were you polite to everyone in the office?

* Were you prepared?

* Were you dressed appropriately?

* Did you carry on an appropriate conversation?

* Did you follow up when and how you said you would?

You set the tone at the first meeting and the expectation for that behavior to continue.

From your approach, which I assume will be consummately professional, you create the expectation that when you do take the order that you will make it right and that you will ensure it is delivered. So customers expect to have a good experience with you.

Customers and prospects want you to spend their time well. To do that, you must establish a trust level that balances appropriate time for conversation, time for your questions, and time for their questions.

Salespeople are well trained in selling their products, but not in building the rapport that will help sell the product. It may help to remember that rapport-building takes time and patience. You build rapport by establishing trust, by doing what you say you will do when you say you will do it, and by being authentic.

GUIDEPOST 11:
Be honest and candid in all communications.

If you are meeting with a prospect, it's valuable to determine up front if this individual is a serious buyer or not. While pursuing what turns out to be a dead end might be inconvenient for you, prospects expect you not to waste their time. To distinguish between a serious buyer and someone who's "just looking," simply ask.

For example, most people are very uncomfortable talking about price or money with a prospect. However, if you begin your conversation by asking about budget, you can figure out right away if someone is serious about your product. Remember, this is business, and anyone who runs a profitable business knows that money is part of the discussion.

Also ask about timing. It may be that the organization is just looking right now but plans to buy in the first quarter of next year. Or it may be that they are simply curious but nowhere near procurement.

Everybody buys the way they want to buy. That may or not be the way you *want* to sell. So who do you suppose needs to change for that to work? It's up to you to adjust to how the buyer wants to buy. And if that doesn't work for you, you need to work on attracting more of the type of customers you work best with. Here are some questions to ask yourself:

Who is your most satisfied customer?

* Why is he satisfied with you?
* How do you meet and exceed expectations?

Who is the customer you most enjoy working with?

* Do you just like working with him because he's become a friend?
* Do you like him just because he gives you the biggest purchase orders?
* Do you like him because his company's orders have the highest profit margin?
* Why do you really like him and his company?
* What does he do for your business?
* How do you meet and exceed his expectations?

Answer these questions, and you will be able to clearly identify a good prospect for you.

Expectations That Lead to Repeat Business

Whether a customer decides to continue to do business with you depends on the sales cycle—meaning, indeed, a cycle. Customers expect to hear from you after the sale. You may need to follow up on some small detail. You may send a thank you. You may call to just check in or say hello. Either way, your behavior after the sale is being scrutinized as closely as your behavior before the sale. It says everything about the authenticity of the relationship between you and your clients.

PROOF POSITIVE.

I was having lunch with a group of colleagues at a national sales training conference a few years ago when one woman turned to a fellow salesperson from her same company and said, "Do you see that guy over there in the blue shirt, wearing the argyle tie? I feel like I should know him, but I'm drawing a blank."

Her co-worker took a look, replied with a chuckle. "Is that so?" she said as the man in question passed our table and shot them both a professional, yet cool, "Hello."

"That's the CEO from your largest account last year. He's one of the speakers this afternoon. You'll be delighted to hear that he's talking about "Relationship Building.""

Everyone at our table was speechless as the woman turned as red as the scarlet blazer she was wearing.

Your Company's Expectations of You

Sometimes the internal sale is harder than the external sale. Your company believes in its products or services 100 percent. Because of this, they theoretically expect you to succeed 100 percent of the time. In many companies, salespeople are among the highest paid of all employees, and management rightly expects them to earn that money.

The company also reasonably expects some level of reporting from you on what you are doing so it can adjust its company-wide forecasts accordingly.

One of the biggest services you can provide for your company is bringing in news from customers in the field. You are in a position to report valuable feedback—about product quality, differentiation, company reputation, or the competition. You can contribute to planning resources and product development by relaying what you hear from customers about what they are missing or will need in the future.

Your Coworkers' Expectations of You

You already know the stereotype people attach to sales professionals. You are the last one in the office in the morning, the first one leaving for home. You might be leaving early to close a big deal, but then again, you are probably out playing golf or schmoozing clients. And of course, while you're out having a "good time," everyone else is busy doing "real" work.

Hate that reputation? It's up to you to reset those expectations. The fact of the matter is that the business doesn't run unless sales happen and revenue comes in. Reminding co-workers of this is not likely to win you any friends; however, honoring how they support your success in sales by what they are doing in the background to make your job easier will definitely win friends.

GUIDEPOST 12:
Understand the role and importance of your company and co-workers in your success.

FIELD STUDIES

* What are your expectations of your clients?
* Which clients aren't meeting those expectations, and is there something you can do to change that?
* Or can you change your expectations?
* Or are they not a good match for you and your company?

NEW TRAVELER TIPS

List the expectations you believe your customers have of you. For each expectation, describe how that expectation was set. What does your sales material say? What impressions will customers have visiting your website? What do you say on that first sales call—a time when so many expectations are set? Study this list for any expectations you know are not currently being met.

SEASONED CLIMBER CHALLENGE

Are there some "disconnects" between what your company is delivering and the reasonable expectations of your customers? Are your delivery times slower than they should be for your industry? Are your terms more restrictive? Is the quality of the product all it should be?

It's easy to be angry about these things and go on selling anyway. But the sales pro knows his or her job is to advocate for the reasonable expectations of the customer and push the company to stellar performance.

Have you done all you can do to intelligently and thoughtfully bring this information to your company in the right forum? Have you been part of the solution?

ASK DEB

Q: All the other companies in my industry give standard three-day delivery, but my company still delivers in seven days. Although we have a superior product and I think our service is superior in all other ways, my prospects all expect a faster delivery time. Management says it takes seven days to create a better, more customized product, but it is hard to get customers to listen. Any suggestions about how to handle this?

A: *WOW! That's quite a discrepancy in delivery time. First thing I would do is to make sure that you are communicating with your management team what your customers are saying. Remember, you are management's eyes and ears on the street.*

Second, if it actually takes your company four days longer to create the product, then work to understand what it is that is happening in those four additional days. This is not just about delivery; we live in the age of things getting delivered around the world by tomorrow every day. And this is a norm, not an exception.

So the four extra days, I hope, is about additional processes that ensure higher quality, better performance, and increased reliability. Once you understand the reason it takes four additional days, you can effectively communicate the difference between you and your competition and help your customers understand the value you are adding. Those extra four days may save them money because they reduce failures, returns, and all the other headaches that go along with faulty product. This, then, is your competitive advantage rather than a competitive liability.

And a customer who realizes a competitive advantage because of your efforts is likely to be a valued customer for years to come.

Want more help on your journey?

See www.TheFieldGuideToSales.com for The Landscape Workbook

YOUR TRAVELING COMPANIONS

CHAPTER 5

It wouldn't be a very rewarding trip if you were traveling alone. Understanding how to build and sustain dynamic, authentic, and profitable relationships is an important survival skill for all sales professionals.

We've already talked about why playing well with others is important; now we'll look at how to make it happen.

YOU Are What You Sell

No matter what else you're selling, you are really selling you.

Your job as a salesperson is to develop connections that foster relationships that allow you to offer goods and services. In the process, you will find out if what you have is valuable to the potential customers. Often, YOU are your company to your customers, and you must accept that some people will want to buy from you, and some people won't.

It's about creating a long-term relationship where you create the opportunity for somebody to buy from you multiple times without your having to "sell" to them.

YOU Are What They Buy

A new sales relationship is like any brand-new relationship. The prospect knows nothing about you, and vice versa. You both may be open to moving forward, but nothing happens without communication, trust, and expectations.

GUIDEPOST 13:
Customers buy you before they buy your product or service.

Sales is about creating a relationship where none existed before. Everything else is customer service

Start building the relationship by focusing on the customer or prospect. Encourage that person to talk about himself, his company, his vision for success. Beyond gathering information, the reason for starting here is to establish the trust that leads to open communication. Because I truly like people, I work to make them feel comfortable; as a result, they share information with me. I want them to know they can trust me with that information and that I want to understand what they need because of my genuine interest in helping them. For many salespeople, this is intuitive.

Getting There From Here

The Rule of 250 says that each of us knows, on average, 250 people. And for every one of the 250 people you know, each of those people knows 250 people.

This rule is based on the concept of six degrees of separation—the idea that we are at most a distance of six other people from connecting with anyone in the world. *Some theorists even argue that with the explosion of technology, the number of degrees has dropped to three or four.* Simply by asking "Whom do you know?" and "Whom do they know?" you could meet anyone living in the world today.

Whom do you really want to know? Look at your list of contacts and try to make connections that lead you to people on your list of suspects. Then ask those contacts if they'd be willing to introduce you. The great news is that one of the ways people most like to help others is by creating this type of connection. The people you know want to help you—all you have to do is ask.

PROOF POSITIVE

I had a client who would find ways each year to avoid a trip home to visit his extended family for the holidays. I prodded him to go, saying, "Grandma is not going to be here forever, you know" whenever he complained.

After managing to avoid making the trip for several years, he finally decided he had better just suck it up and go. Monday morning following the holiday week, I was greeted by an ecstatic voice mail from him telling me that the one person he had been trying to meet for years turned out to be a business associate of his uncle!

The secret to your success is right in front of you and all around you. If the only two things you implement this year are to create your rolling forecast and develop new prospects through family, friends and colleagues, I guarantee you a record year.

That First Step is a Doozey

Even the most ambitious and natural salespeople get nervous about making that first call.

To lessen the tension, have an objective for each sales call, whether it's via phone or in person. Think through an objective and a desired and follow-up action.

Picking up the phone or walking through the door to create that first impression takes resolve and persistence. It's anyone's guess what will happen; you may interrupt the smooth flow of someone's day, or you may be the best thing that will happen to him the whole month.

Because we live in a high-tech world, it's likely your first phone call will be met by voice mail. Don't hang up! Take the opportunity to leave valuable information on the recording.

But wait! Don't pick up the phone before you think of what you want to impart that is engaging or interesting enough to prompt a return call. Before the call, create a script—not the kind you read like a robot, but the kind that gives you cues on how the message should flow. Your script should incorporate the thought process for what you want to say so you are not making things up as you go along. You won't read your script word for word, but it will guide what you say; most important, you won't forget any of the key points you want to convey.

And don't forget to let your passion for what you do come through in your voice.

GUIDEPOST 14:
Focus on the customer, not the sale.

Given the volume of calls your suspect, prospect, or customer probably receives in a day, there's a good chance your call may not be returned. But you're resilient; don't give up.

Give it another try and then another, each time leaving another intelligent, valuable piece of information, or asking a question about something you know to be a challenge in that person's business or industry.

This type of message illustrates that you understand something critical about this person's business and that you have successfully created viable solutions. Isn't that better than simply leaving your name and number?

Maybe the prospect will answer the fourth time you dial or call you back the following week. Maybe your customer has been busy traveling or putting out fires. If you have set it up right, he already knows several key points about your product or service from your messages by the time you and he have that first conversation.

In sales, it is said that it generally takes seven interactions to close a sale. We all have stories about working for years for a single significant sale or of it's happening on the first communication because we called at exactly the right time.

Take it step-by-step. You don't know if this sale will take seven days or seven years. Start by working toward one initial objective. Perhaps you've reached the client, but they say they can't meet with you in the next few weeks. If an objective to set a meeting can't be met, then have a secondary position, perhaps to have him agree to your contacting him in a week to see if his schedule might be more open then.

With every call, email or meeting, you are exhibiting your intention to further the relationship in some way. You are calling for a productive result—to get someone's name or number, to get an appointment, or even to get a signed contract.

Contrary to popular opinion, sales is about giving, first to create solid relationships by helping others. But there is another relationship that needs continual nurturing—the relationship with yourself. How about giving to you through education and support?

Hire a Trail Guide

Sales can be a lonely endeavor. Whether you're working for yourself or you work for somebody else, it's part of the sales mentality to say, "I can do it myself," or "If it's going to get done, it's up to me to do it."

And then there is that nagging feeling that the win—the sale—won't mean as much if you are helped. The typical salesperson loves feeling he did it all himself. Many salespeople find it hard to admit that, however high their level of expertise, there is always something new to learn. We come to our sales calls as experts in our products, and we often think of ourselves as experts in human nature as well.

Finally, there is a feeling among many salespeople that you've either got "it" or you don't. You're either a natural-born salesperson or you're not; in other words, sales skills can't be taught. Not true!

Some companies require or allow salespeople to take continuing sales training. If you're lucky enough to work at such a company, take as much training as you can. But a true sales professional will go beyond what is offered and seek out what information or opportunity fills a need for them. *(Like reading this book.)*

PROOF POSITIVE

Several years ago, I finally decided to stop going it alone and hire a sales coach. This decision created a safe place for me to come and say what was the truth, the whole truth, to someone I knew I could count on to give me support and encouragement and hit me with any truth I needed to hear.

For the past three years, I've budgeted several thousand dollars a year for education and professional development. I use these funds for both traditional training and mentoring with my coach. I consider this money an investment, not an expense. The result is that I have grown my business, changed and added product offerings, and become more profitable.

GUIDEPOST 15:
Don't go it alone.

I believe sales is a calling. But as with many callings, it isn't always easy to discern the right path. Working with someone who has already faced the challenges ahead of you and lived to tell about it makes it easier to explore how you want to manifest your life journey through the activity of sales, as opposed to sales being simply something you do for a living.

A coach or mentor is somebody you can talk to and be open with and who can help you with your relationships: with yourself, with your confidence, with your clients, and with your co-workers.

PROOF POSITIVE

Another great source of support is professional groups comprising people who aren't your competitors but professional colleagues —people who do what you do and know the stresses intimately.

I belong to a professional group that includes people who are in other fields—marketing, law, banking, investments, real estate—who understand what I do, refer others to me on a regular basis, and who have helped and supported me for more than fifteen years.

FIELD STUDIES

Sources of sales training, coaching, mentoring

- www.The-Sales-Company.com (Debbie Mrazek)
- www.StrausUSA.com (My coach—Steve Straus)
- www.WinReferrals.com (Genie Fuller)
- www.smei.org (Sales and Marketing Executives International)

NEW TRAVELER TIPS

Put the Rule of 250 into practice. Make a list (or print out your contacts if in a database and label them) of people you know in these categories:

- Family
- Friends—neighbors, church, school, college, clubs
- Professional Organizations—business
- Volunteer Groups—in the community, for an event, in your neighborhood
- Alumni Associations—college, military, fraternity
- Sports—from childhood to now, the gym
- Community—church, arts, doctor, any business or service you frequent
- Work—previous or current coworkers

Now, think of this in another way: Based on what you know about the best companies you work with, think of ten other companies doing just what these companies are doing. Who would you like to meet at these new companies? Can you connect anyone on your Rule of 250 lists to any of these new suspect companies?

SEASONED CLIMBER CHALLENGE

Are you doing everything you can to develop new relationships and keep the ones you have?

* For each prospect, have you established rapport with the decision-maker?
* Have you adequately qualified your prospects so you know they need what you sell?
* Is the prospect company the right size to benefit from and be able to afford your product or service?
* Can you provide the product or service in the time frame required?

ASK DEB

Q: How can I find a consistent source of referrals to fill my pipeline?

A: *When someone provides a good service to you—your banker, your accounting firm, your mechanic, a restaurant—do you automatically provide him or her with referrals? Probably not. But don't you want your friends and family to have the benefit of great service and products, too?*

Yes, of course, but most people just don't think about it. When we ask for a referral from someone, the request is often much too general. We ask if they know "anyone" who would appreciate our service, but "anyone" is too broad and people don't know what to do with it.

But if you ask, "Do you know anyone who has a law practice that deals with family disputes or litigation?" or "Do you know anyone who has children who are teenagers now and will be going to college in four to five years?" they can more easily respond.

The fact is happy clients who like you would like to help you grow your business, but it's generally harder for them to help you if you ask a question that's too broad.

Another great source of referrals is a group of referral partners (www.WinReferrals.com). You must invest the time to understand specifically what they do and who their ideal clients are. They, in turn, invest in learning what you do and the attributes of a great client for you. It is like having your own personal marketing group working for you all day, every day.

If you don't like helping others, this solution probably will not work for you. It's designed to be a two-way street. When everyone is working together for the good of one another, business will happen again and again and again; the group begins to resemble a strong piece of fabric.

Being selective is key in picking referral partners. You're not going to a Chamber of Commerce event and exchanging a raft of business cards! It takes time to develop and maintain a referral group, but it's time well spent.

Want more help on your journey?

See www.TheFieldGuideToSales.com for the Your Traveling Companions Workbook

OUTBOUND COMMUNICATIONS

CHAPTER 6

Effective communication skills are necessary to any team effort, whether scaling a mountain or orchestrating a sale. To hone your survival skills, start by taking a look at the messages you're sending out and how you're sending them.

The professional salesperson must master three major components of communication:

1. Listening to customers, including watching for body language
2. Questioning and listening to find out what they want and what their concerns are
3. Establishing the connection between their needs and your products and services

In this chapter, we'll focus on the active, outbound parts of communication: providing and requesting information. In the next chapter, we'll turn things around to cover the inbound side of communication: listening.

Take the Lead

One of the simplest ways companies can attract and keep clients is to properly communicate what the company will deliver and then deliver it. It takes a while for your external client to decide if he or she is open to the conversation about doing business with you, so, it's worth spending some time preparing to make a great first impression.

It will be up to you to set the tone for the interaction and start the conversation. One of the best openings is a friendly, open, personal question.

Too often, salespeople are interested only in conveying what they want to say about their product or service, which is why many buyers loathe salespeople; they don't ask questions or seem genuinely interested in the client as a person, but instead see him only as a buyer. Your clients are people first, clients second.

When people are new in sales, they are so focused on getting the product information right that they don't think to ask about the customer. They're not conversing; they're reciting.

And when salespeople begin to understand that they need to ask questions, they are so focused on asking their questions and moving on to reciting their product information that it becomes a pointed interrogation rather than a conversation.

Nothing says "amateur" and is more uncomfortable for the recipient than being asked a list of preplanned questions that continue on even if the answers the prospect gives to one question make the other questions on the salesperson's prepared list irrelevant to the situation or the prospect.

Such an approach leaves the customer with nowhere to go but no.

It comes down to motive. What's the motive? What's the objective? If salespeople are truly motivated only by money, the customer will sense it immediately. Are you just trying to say what you want to say and make the sale, or are you really interested in helping the client?

GUIDEPOST 16:
Take the lead in relationship building.

PROOF POSITIVE

If you think clients don't see motive, try this: Take a look back at any thank-you notes or emails you've received from customers. If your experience is like mine, customers almost never thank you for the great prices. They thank you for what you genuinely brought to the table—things such as:

- helping them with a stressful situation
- being an advocate and friend
- providing excellent service and follow-up
- going above and beyond their expectations

Moving Forward

Although a conversation typically involves at least two participants, the salesperson must take hold of the reins and determine the direction so the interaction is as productive as possible. You are the one trained for the sales experience, and when the prospect trusts you to be in charge, great things can happen.

I've had clients say to me, "Do you realize in the first five minutes we talked, I told you more than I've told thirty other people this month?"

Asking open-ended questions and listening for certain words will give clues about unarticulated problems. Maybe you hear that they are back-ordered on a product line so their productivity in that area isn't what they would like it to be. Your questions should follow the words that reflect the area of opportunity—something like "You're concerned with productivity" and "Okay, how so?" Such open-ended questions allow you to continue going deeper and deeper until you find out and pinpoint the customer's actual problem.

The sad truth is that a lot of salespeople don't do that. They start out with bold promises and never get to the heart of the connection between what they sell and the solution to the customer's problem.

Using a consultative questioning technique helps the customer express his thoughts out loud and uncover what is really going on. There is a real dialogue, not just a superficial chat. The great salesperson takes the customer on a continuing journey.

GUIDEPOST 17:
Seek answers that will lead you to the problem.

What Makes You So Special?

It is essential that you communicate four messages when you talk with a prospect:

1. **Who are you?** If I were an advertising executive, I could say, "I'm an advertising account rep." But wouldn't it be more engaging if I said something descriptive of the benefits I offer someone? So instead, I'd introduce myself as "a promotional powerhouse." With an opening like that, he's certain to want to hear more.

   I have a colleague who is a marketing consultant — or rather "an alchemist of words, pictures and plans." One of the services she offers her clients is coaching on making an attention-getting "elevator pitch." Typically, this version of who you are and what you do is no longer than 30 seconds. The intention is to give people enough information to determine if they want to know more. Here are a few of the tweaks she has created:

   For a travel agent specializing in cruises: "I'm an escape artist."

   For a graphics designer: "I'm an architect of lasting impressions."

   For a computer support consultant: "I'm the one to call before you get out the sledgehammer."

   For a financial planner: "I'm a fiscal fitness trainer."

2. **What do you sell?** What do you really sell, and what is a customer going to get from you? The same concepts of describing who you are in an accurate yet unexpected way apply. If you are an insurance agent, are you selling insurance policies or are you selling peace of mind? You could say, "I sell insurance" but why not say, "I help people sleep better at night." Remember, you don't just sell a product or service—you sell what you can do to make their lives and businesses better.

3. **Who is your client?** Aim for your ideal client. Who is he? How does he act? For example, I know an investment advisor who says: "I work with nice, wealthy, patient people." Sounds kind of elementary, but it's effective because people remember it, and there is NO question about who she's looking for. She doesn't work with fun people who aren't rich, and vice versa.

4. **What is different about you?** Why are you different from everyone else who sells what you sell? Tell me why YOU are unique and

entice me to want to know more about you. What am I going to miss out on by NOT knowing you?

PROOF POSITIVE

An accountant told me a story about one of his prospects. The accountant said he introduced himself and his product and felt pretty good about what he had said. He talked about how great his firm is, how much education the partners have, and the depth and breadth of experience his professionals have with the prospect's industry.

When he was finished, the company owner asked, "Do you realize that everyone who has come through that door has said the same things? What makes you different?"

The accountant, good at thinking on his feet, said, "Well, we do what we say we will, and we are a lot of fun to do business with. We aren't stuffy and uptight." That was just the difference he needed to get the job.

Body Language

Have you ever observed a truly great salesperson talking to a client? Even sitting still and not saying a word, he exudes focus. How does this make the customer feel? "Like I hired a consultant with the right resources and answers who is focused only on me and my problems."

More than half of the messages you communicate are non-verbal. The same thing is true with your customers. So how you say it is as important as what you say.

It's eye contact, gestures, inflection, tone, and posture. It's being authentic—showing who you really are—not some façade you hide behind. It pays to be authentic because body language rarely lies.

Follow the Scent of Opportunity

Every opportunity isn't the perfect opportunity.

In fact, a lot more is going to go wrong than is going to go right. After all, we and our clients are only human. In addition to that, so many factors impact our days and our decision-making. John Lennon was right: Life is what happens when you've made other plans.

It wouldn't be surprising if you got angry and defensive when things went wrong or simply not according to plan. But would you rather be right/inconvenienced/perfect/fill in the blank... or make the sale?

PROOF POSITIVE

It took two months for me to get an initial meeting with one prospect I was interested in. We scheduled and rescheduled meetings twelve times in eight weeks.

Just when I had all but given up, deciding he was just too nice to simply tell me he wasn't interested, he called and requested a meeting as soon as possible. He had a problem.

His assistant gave me the choice between the only two available open slots—each two weeks out—either 1 p.m. or 4 p.m. on Friday. I chose 4 p.m.

I knew he was serious about doing business by what he said on the phone and the way he said it. I gave some thought to how I wanted to approach this meeting and as part of my preparation, I put a thermos of margaritas, two glasses, and a bag of ice in a bag, along with my presentation materials.

When I walked in at 4 p.m. on Friday, I said, "Finally meeting after twelve reschedules is worth celebrating. Do you like margaritas?" He said yes, so I took out the thermos and put it on his desk. If only you could have seen his face!

The meeting was unforgettable. Bringing the margaritas communicated there were no hard feelings on my part.

After we talked and I presented my solution to his problem, he was so relieved that he volunteered he had recently bought another company and asked if we needed to wait until next year to get these people into the new system as well. I answered immediately: "Absolutely not!"

The moral of the story? Don't let impatience or frustration cost you a sale—or more important, a relationship.

Back Away From the Scent of Skunks

There will be situations when it is appropriate for you to say, "I value this relationship but I don't see a way for me to support you fully with what you need, but I'd like to stay in touch in case things change down the road."

It's not about throwing business away; it's about walking away when a prospect isn't a good fit.

The best customer has a strategic plan. Their management team is rock-solid, open, and communicative. They want win/win negotiations with their vendors and partners, and they make decisions quickly.

The customer who isn't right for you is secretive. If you win, they lose, so they work hard to make sure you don't win. They make decisions bureaucratically that are based on price, not value.

When you're desperate and don't have a big pipeline and you've got to sell something, you go after whichever customers will take you. And logic dictates 50 percent will be the best ones and 50 percent the worst.

GUIDEPOST 18:
Be certain of what differentiates you, and don't be afraid to boldly state it.

Strive to communicate what you have to offer so clearly that customers who aren't a fit will recognize it. This will leave you with a solid customer base you are confident you can serve well for the long haul.

Everyone Paddle! (in the Same Direction)

Effective communication with your boss and co-workers is critical to your success as well. You are all in the same boat; you can only make progress if everyone is paddling in the same direction.

* Expect respect and give it—unreservedly—along with all the information you have. Withholding information from colleagues is a surefire way of making sure you all fail.

* Give the benefit of the doubt in any situation. Others may be looking out for you more than you think.

* Serve as a teacher whenever possible. You may open up doors of possibility others haven't considered.

FIELD STUDIES

Watch salespeople in action. Go to an electronics store or car dealership or call an 800 number. Listen for the words, be aware of the attitude, and see how you feel as the customer. How much of the conversation is about your needs, and how much is "pitch"?

NEW TRAVELER TIPS

Take the answer to these four questions and blend them into three or four sentences—write just enough to be clear about what you do—remembering benefits—and being lively enough to spark interest.

* Who are you?
* What do you sell?
* Who buys your product or service?
* What is unique about you?

SEASONED CLIMBER CHALLENGE

Remember a time when communication with a prospect or client got off course. What did you do or say to change the situation? Were you able to approach the customer and answer the hard questions? Did you do it with humility and grace? Were you able to turn the tide back to a trusting relationship? What do you wish you had done differently?

ASK DEB

Q: How and when do I ask for and use testimonials or endorsements from clients?

A: *If you have never asked for testimonials, do it today!*

A client's words will always be more powerful than yours to another potential client.

The best time to ask for a testimonial is when you go back to the client after the sale to follow up. If they have shared with you how pleased they are with your product or service and how it worked for them, ask if they would be willing to share those thoughts with others. You may be a bit nervous about asking, but do it anyway. Oftentimes, I find people are amazed at all the good things the client will say and who they will say it to if you just ask!

Once you have their words/testimonials, share them with other prospects or those you meet so they can understand what you do. Use the testimonials on your website, in your marketing materials, in your voice mail messages, on the back of your business card, and when you are networking.

For example, next time you introduce yourself to someone and they ask what you do say, "My name is Marcus with ABC-Inc, and our customers say we _____." Most salespeople say, "My name is _____ with _____, and we have the best _____ ever known to man that can do everything." People tune out when you go into a sales pitch, but they tune in to what your product or service has done for others.

OUTBOUND COMMUNICATIONS

You want what you do to be memorable and easy for others to understand so they can tell two people who tell two people who tell ... you get the idea! It's about connecting and telling, not selling!

Keep your focus on your business and your clients and the great stories they have to share about you. Make sure you're sharing those stories so the word gets out about you and your company. Business will flock to your door!

Want more help on your journey?

See www.TheFieldGuideToSales.com for the Outbound Communications Workbook

INBOUND COMMUNICATION

CHAPTER 7

Once you've polished your outbound messages, shift your focus to incoming messages. Whether you are poised on the edge of a cliff or working on a sale, being able to hear the other individuals around you and understand what they are communicating, directly and indirectly, is critical to your survival.

As noted in the last chapter, sales communication is a three-step process: listening, watching for body language, and talking and using body language. In this chapter, we will focus on listening.

Learning to listen means learning the patience to be quiet.

The average person can talk at a rate of roughly 260 to 300 words per minute. Most people can listen and absorb information at six or seven times that rate. That's why we are so prone to mental multitasking. We read the paper, watch TV, eat dinner, and think about what's coming up at the office tomorrow or what we need to do with the kids later this evening—all at the same time! Just knowing our brains work this way shows us that unless we develop skills otherwise, we are prone mentally to do too many things at once, and none of them well. To stop this process takes an intention to do so and a *lot of practice*.

The greatest gift you can give your client (*and anyone else, for that matter*) is to be present, to be absolutely focused just on them and what they are saying; not to let your brain wander off to the myriad of other things going on at the same time.

While this can be challenging, it is essential. Listening helps build rapport with the client. Giving the client time to talk and feel heard will help that client really listen to you later. You are setting the tone for the relationship from the first conversation.

Giving your mouth a rest allows your mind to work, taking what you hear as a whole and being better able to process it when the time is right.

GUIDEPOST 19:
Listen at least 60 percent of the time; talk no more than 40 percent of the time.

There is a distinction, of course, between hearing and listening. Hearing is the process of your brain registering a sound that has entered in through your ears. Listening is comprehension; being tuned-in, attentive, and intentional.

Learn to listen in a way that doesn't find you continually thinking about the questions you want to ask next. Whenever you are thinking about the next question you want to ask, you are not really listening to the client.

Silence is not a bad thing. People can be uncomfortable with silence and feel the need to fill in the gaps. Practice being in silence to become more comfortable with it. The silence can be short, just a pause for a few seconds, or it can be much longer, but that pause will show that you are not in a hurry and are really there for the customer. It shows that you care about his comfort and his timetable. The client will appreciate that you are giving them the time to formulate his thoughts. If you rush in to fill the quiet space and start talking, he may never get back to the point he was trying to make, which might have been crucial information for you to know.

The questions you want to ask are those that help you gather information to move the sales process forward; questions that bring you a better understanding of the who, what, where, why, how of the opportunity. Consider preparing these questions ahead of time when you go into a sales call, both as a way to think about what you want to learn, and also as a way to free yourself to fully listen.

Ready, Set, Sshhhhhhh...

While listening may seem to be a passive process, in reality it is anything but. Listening is an active process. Show you are actively listening by doing the following:

* Make eye contact when customers speak.
* Be aware of your posture, how you are sitting or standing.
* Make encouraging gestures, like nodding, leaning forward, smiling.
* Take notes, using whatever method you use to document your meetings.

Active listening means giving your customer visible encouragement and offering assurance that you are paying attention and are interested in his concerns, goals, and what he has to say in general.

It will be obvious to your customer whether you are not listening fully, but only listening to get ammunition for saying something yourself. It isn't easy to train yourself to actively listen, but when you are, doors will open and solutions will present themselves.

As humans, whenever we listen, we naturally sort and categorize what we hear so we can effectively remember and respond. When you listen to your customers, it's important to learn to listen for all the parts of the message and leave responding for a separate time.

When we listen by getting ready to analyze and respond, then we aren't listening to the whole message. We prejudge everything we are hearing and categorize it into where *we think* it fits in with what we've already heard. It means we only listen to about 20 percent of the message.

This is particularly a problem when the customer is talking as a means of thinking about sorting through what they want and need. We solve the problem in our heads before he finishes his explanation instead of helping him sort through the problem and then connect to the solution.

Your watching skills must be developed along with your listening skills. As you learn to listen without categorizing, also begin to listen and note what you see—especially what is in synch with what you are hearing and what is not. Watch your customer's body language. Sometimes what the body is saying is much more telling than the words. The words may be nice but if the body is stiff, the arms crossed, and the jaw set, you can be sure there is more to the story.

Eye contact is important, of course, but make your gaze natural. It should be comfortable for you (and for them). Don't stare incessantly. Break eye contact occasionally by looking down at your page to write notes, or reviewing a point they just made.

Be at ease and relaxed without crossing that fine line to being too familiar. Your client is not your best friend, and while you always want to be yourself, be your best self. Even if you'd like to develop a more lasting or personal relationship with the client, it isn't appropriate to start that way. When you are at ease with yourself, you are much more likely to be at ease with the customer. Respecting boundaries will help.

A habit of familiarity many of us get into is to finish another person's sentences. This generally frustrates clients because it just means you are taking over the conversation and not really listening. **Always** let them complete their thoughts; above all, do not interrupt.

PROOF POSITIVE

I mentored someone new to sales who was nothing if not enthusiastic. She accompanied me several times to observe and assist with sales presentations. She made a great impression on everyone we met, was respectfully silent during critical conversations, and was, in general, delightful to work with.

Then came the day for her to go out on her own. She had been "courting" a client for several weeks and was about to close the sale.

While I anxiously waited for her to return to the office with the news of her first sale, my phone rang. It was her client.

I gingerly asked how everything had gone. "Well," said the gentleman, laughing in a fatherly tone, "I tried to give her the sale, I really did, but she wouldn't let me get a word in edgewise, so perhaps you could let her know that, and send her back tomorrow with the paperwork."

Another habit of poor listeners is interrupting. They editorialize midstream. They solve problems out loud before hearing all the variables. They talk too much. They are judgmental.

When you are actively listening, you are listening for everything as well as listening for something. Listen selectively. This may sound like a bad thing, but it's not. A trained listener reads between the lines. The client is saying one thing to you, but you hear that he or she is saying something else. If you are new in sales, this is sometimes hard to discern, but it will become second nature in time. Listening between the lines is a valuable skill. Listen to discover who this person is and what is important to him, what is challenging him, and if what you do is a good fit to help with that challenge.

We all know people buy for different reasons. Some people buy intuitively; they just feel good about something, they have an inner knowing, a belief that it will work. Some people buy based on analysis and logic. Listening to the client's words and examples of when something didn't work in the past will help you understand what the client needs to feel comfortable when making the buying decision.

GUIDEPOST 20:
Build relationships through discerning your clients' values, challenges and goals.

Effective communication allows you to develop and maintain rapport with customers that builds relationships and long-term business deals.

The Four Types of Listeners

You may think you are one of those listeners who can multitask and doesn't need to listen fully as I've suggested because you are a seasoned veteran of the sales process and you know how to do it all. Through all the sales training I've done, I've discovered that there are really only four types of listeners, and the four fit the acronym SALE:

* **S**cavengers
* **A**ttention-Challenged
* **L**iteral
* **E**mpathetic

Scavengers are just looking for scraps of information about what the client needs. They pick up less than 20 percent of the entire message because they are listening only to decide what to say next. Scavengers typically don't listen between the lines. This tells the client he or she is just a sales number and that his or her problems are not really important to the salesperson.

The **attention-challenged** can't seem to focus on the client. They don't look the customer in the eye, or their gaze is continually distracted by something else going on in the room. They are so busy shuffling papers or showing the clients their wonderful sales materials that they completely forget to focus and listen to the client. Usually the client gives up and lets the salesperson drive the process while silently vowing never to do business with this person.

Literal salespeople listen to the client and acknowledge exactly what is said. They don't listen between the lines and don't look for clues of what the client may not be revealing. They accept whatever the client says he needs, without wondering if there is more to the story, or more information that would help them find a better solution together. They may hurry the client through the process, leaving an untold amount of dollars on the table and a dissatisfied client with a problem still not completely solved.

Empathetic salespeople are the success stories. If you want to be a truly great sales professional, really listen first, create rapport and gain the trust of the client—not as a ploy to get sales, but because you genuinely care. Leave an ample number of silent pauses to allow the client to complete thoughts. Smile and nod; maintain eye contact.

Give and Let Give

Perhaps the main benefit of empathetic, active listening is that you've modeled behavior your customer can mirror. If you lean in, nod or shake your head, your clients are more likely to do the same, giving you tremendous clues when he is excited about what you are saying.

You can help your clients communicate better with you by doing four things:

* Speak their language.
* Say something worth hearing.
* Coax them out of their natural habitat; for example, meet a client at a local coffee shop instead of at his office.
* Establish that what you are saying will be valuable to them.

PROOF POSITIVE

One of my favorite clients had her desk in the midst of the office, which was actually more of a showroom. She liked it that way because her landscape equipment repair business was based on walk-in traffic and she liked to greet the customers.

While this was an excellent way for her to build relationships with her customers, it also gave her the feeling that she always had to be at her desk, even during our meetings. As much as I liked her, I hated meeting with her. Invariably, phones, customers, vendors, and employees distracted her from the work we were trying to do. In her office, she was conditioned to be tuned-in to everything going on around her, and our "meetings" dragged on, with little being accomplished and ending with our business undone.

After a string of unproductive meetings, I suggested we meet at a local bagel shop. She arrived ten minutes late, looking harried and scattered. After decompressing with coffee and friendly conversation, we got down to business. We wrapped up everything in under thirty minutes.

As we parted, she said, "I just accomplished more in a half hour than I get done in most days. Thank you for kidnapping me."

Tune Your Receiver to the Strongest Signal

Once you've completed the first phase of the communications process, listening by just listening, you can thoughtfully respond—mirroring tempo and style and finding just the right words to connect with the customer's needs and desires.

The biggest problem for most salespeople when they finally get through the listening phase is to assume that now it's their turn to talk, so they make up for lost time by talking for 20 minutes straight. Do this, and you will completely unravel any rapport or trust you have created.

Your 40 percent (or less) of the talking should be all about answers—answering questions and seeking answers. Just be careful not to grill the client. The sales process works much better when it feels like a natural conversation.

If you feel like you are talking too much, or feel pressured to talk because the customer isn't, stop, refocus, and then ask an open-ended question to get the conversation moving again.

GUIDEPOST 21:
Be genuinely interested, not just interested until you make the sale.

Listening is a skill set that must be developed. There is no substitute for challenging yourself to become a better listener and practicing the necessary skills. And the more you practice, the more this skill becomes a second skin. It's rewarding when it all comes together and you realize you are naturally getting much more value and information from the conversations you have with your clients.

Suppose your client has just started to talk about her budget for the year. Did you just hear the word budget, or did you hear that they have less budget this year than they had last year? What if you heard that they have no budget now, in June, but will have additional budget in the fourth quarter? Do you continue selling, or do you adjust your course accordingly to continue building rapport, knowing that relationships lead to long-term profitable sales?

If you can learn to listen well, and do it consistently, you can close more business in less time. And if you can close business in less time, how much more business could you do in a year?

The unfortunate and sad truth is that many salespeople do not truly care about their clients. They care only about the order, the deal, and the commission. These salespeople tend not to last at one place very long. They move around a lot and never understand why they don't have satisfied customers and aren't making the money they'd like to. You can't fake sincerity.

So what can good listening generate for you and your bottom line?

FIELD STUDIES

Think about times when you really felt heard by others. Consider how it made you feel. Did you think or do anything differently as a result? Can you do that for your customers?

NEW TRAVELER TIPS

Try this role-playing exercise with a professional colleague or coach: You play the salesperson, and your colleague plays your customer. Have the customer talk and then stop every few minutes and you, as the salesperson, tell the customer what you heard. Your colleague will then tell you what you missed. At the end, have your colleague tell you what you didn't ask, but should have, and what it felt like to be your customer.

Your customers are nice people, and they won't tell you that you didn't listen well or that they don't feel understood. What they will tell you is no, you do not get the order.

While worthwhile, this is not an easy exercise for most salespeople, but if you do it more than once, it will get easier.

SEASONED CLIMBER CHALLENGE

Do you use these questions in your conversations with clients and then stop and listen?

- What is the most difficult/best part of your business right now?
- Who do you consider competitors in your industry?
- Have you always been in this type of business?
- How do other people usually find out about your business?
- What would you most like to be different about your business? What can you effectively do about it?
- Where do you currently get most of your business?
- How can I help you with your business?
- Who would you like to meet?
- What is the most exciting piece of business you have ever done? How have you been able to duplicate that success?
- How do you keep up to date in your industry?
- What part does technology play in your business?

ASK DEB

Q: As a natural introvert, should I even think about getting into sales? Are some areas better suited than others, for instance, going into insurance sales instead of real estate sales?

A: *The answer to your question is a definite YES! Sales can be an absolutely wonderful career for an introvert. Who is better at truly listening?*

No matter what it is you sell, the customer or client should be the focus. Unfortunately, so many salespeople think THEY are the focus and so do not really make the sales presentations with the customer or client in mind. They make presentations, not conversation.

If you sell around understanding the customer's issue, problem, difficulty, or need, you are better able to formulate what solution you can offer with your product or service. Customers love it when someone really listens to them and understands what they are dealing with before trying to sell them something.

In answer to your second question about some areas being better suited to introverts than others, I don't really think so. What's important is that you sell something you know and love. Those will always be the easiest things for you to be successful at selling, and that applies whether you are an introvert or an extrovert!

Want more help on your journey?

See www.TheFieldGuideToSales.com for the Inbound Communication Workbook

AWARENESS OF THE ENVIRONMENT

CHAPTER 8

In the wild, the ability to hear a twig snap or notice a fresh bear track can be the difference between life and death. Being aware is your best defense—and offense. When you have gotten your communication skills into shape, put them to the test by responding to your sales environment and its inhabitants.

A Great Set of Binoculars

One of the most important tasks of every salesperson is taking the temperature of the external and internal environment. This may not be in your job description, but it should be.

It's easy for management to overlook how valuable salespeople can be at serving as the eyes and ears of the company. But who better to pay attention to what customers are doing in their businesses, where the industry is going, and what competitors are doing? Salespeople, in their normal course of business, are privy to this vital information every single day.

Every time a prospect or customer says no, some sort of critical feedback is attached. This is especially true for a trained, seasoned salesperson who knows the "no" wasn't about him or her, but about the product or service, reputation of the company for innovation, customer service, or other aspects that go into decision-making.

Technology is effective, but a curious, intuitive salesperson is better at creating connections and understanding nuances. When someone in a company knows about a critical situation with a customer, he can raise awareness by making notes about the situation and the action taken, then share them via email or posting to a company-wide database.

The loss of a good salesperson is a critical loss for the company. Salespeople represent a brain trust that too often is underutilized when making decisions at the highest level.

I have seen companies that, when frustrated with low sales figures, fire an entire sales team. While salespeople may be accountable for bringing in revenue, when they are gone, a company can lose the knowledge database about all the prospects currently in the pipeline, not to mention customers who are with the company because of the salesperson who built the account.

Anyone who thinks salespeople are replaceable by technology needs to pay more attention to the benefits of human awareness and thinking in the business process. A Customer Relationship Management (CRM) system is not a salesperson, and computers and software can't maintain person-to-person relationships.

It is vital to have discussions with your company about the four types of awareness you have about your sales territory:

1. Client awareness
2. Industry/competitor awareness
3. Internal business awareness
4. Self-awareness

Client Awareness

How aware are you of your customers and their businesses? Do you try to stay on the sales path, or do you keep your blinders on, and not actively pay attention to anything that might upset the deal?

The saying "an ounce of prevention is worth a pound of cure" is so critical in sales. If only more salespeople realized that prevention of the situations that take time and jeopardize sales relationships is worth years of cures, they would be more attentive to being prepared up front.

Awareness means paying attention to everything in the environment when you are at a customer's place of business, whether you are talking to him or her in person or on the phone. Is there something you are not noticing?

Is there a clear lack of activity, lots of empty desks? Is there too much activity—chaos and angry people shouting at one another? Define what you are seeing in terms of how it might impact your ability to sustain a long-term relationship with this client.

Read news releases put out by clients and ask questions. Note if there are senior management changes that might signal a change in strategy. Set Google alerts for customers and industry news; visit customer and industry websites often.

One way to increase your awareness is with a direct question: "Why are you looking for this product or service right now?" For example, has the customer just come through a bad experience with a competitor? How can you learn from that dissatisfaction?

You may or may not be able to meet the stringent government standards that stopped your competitors from meeting quality expectations. Better to know sooner rather than later.

Customers are people, and people have quirks and idiosyncrasies. Layer that with personal needs, sensitivities, preferences, and corporate missions, and you end up with multiple agendas from the customer, but one mission for you.

We all know each company has its own set of rules about how things are supposed to get done, but when you are aware, you know there is a whole different culture that dictates how things *really* get done.

Each person has sensitivities about what is appropriate language and dress, what's funny and what isn't, and much more. While you can't possibly avoid every place you could go wrong, dressing appropriately in business attire and being careful with every word you say or speak will take care of the most obvious potential problems.

GUIDEPOST 22:
Be constantly aware of changes in your customers' businesses and the unspoken rules that stay the same.

There isn't an experienced salesperson who hasn't been through an episode where they would have bet their next commission check on a sale that was a sure thing, only to have it fall through at the last moment.

It is critical we know the "why" when these things happen.

* Was it something you said that offended them, worried them, or caused them concern that made them rethink their decision?

* Was it something they heard from a competitor about you or your product or service?

* Was it something that happened when they were working with someone else on your company's staff?
* Was it something they heard about a competitor's faster, better, cheaper model that was just around the corner?
* Was it an encounter with an impatient customer service rep?
* Was it a change in the direction of their business or in their fortunes that made them pull back?

If it was a preventable step or faux pas on your part, then your best option is to admit to the mistake and see what you can do to correct it. Stepping up is your only possible way to get the client back—now or in the future.

What's the worst reason to lose a customer? The reason you don't know. If they disappear as a customer but are still in business, you have to chalk it up to the fact that you didn't establish enough of a trusting relationship with them. Knowing that they were willing to end it and never see you again is a hard pill to swallow, but learn from your mistake and don't repeat it with your other customers.

Regardless of the reason, it is 100 percent up to you to resurrect the relationship, if it can be saved. That Rule of 250 we discussed earlier applies to your customers, too. They have a broad reach to tell others about you and your company. Always handle situations as if they would be reported on the front page of the newspaper *(in the large font above the fold of the paper)* the next day. Take the high road, always, without exception.

If this were easy, we'd have the perfect prescription for success.

We live in a pill-popping, instant-gratification world, and we all want answers that lead us to a fix. Too many salespeople refuse to accept the fact that things sometimes go wrong, or that this might not be the right customer at the right time. They refuse to regroup and move on. Instead, they blithely continue with the sales pitch, completely oblivious to what is going on around them.

You could even deliver an outstanding proposal for a solution that meets and exceeds the customer's stated needs and still not make a sale.

It takes maturity to hang tough, to follow through and close the loop, if not the entire cycle.

Industry/Competitor Awareness

In many industries, there is a constant consolidation and re-invention of companies, meaning that yesterday's competitor could become tomorrow's partner or boss.

Bottom line: NEVER bad-mouth the competition! NEVER bad-mouth anyone!

There are many good reasons to stay in touch with and have positive relationships with competitors. They may occupy a slightly different market niche than yours, and you can refer prospects that aren't right for you to them—making you the hero in the eyes of the customer or prospect. You may not be part of the solution, but you were the one who created and facilitated the solution.

You may be able to work in partnership with a competitor to get a large account, if the resources required are beyond what either one of you could come up with separately. In sales, we say that "50 percent of something is better than a 100 percent of nothing" to describe a rationalization for accepting a lower price, but it also fits this situation. Instead of not being able to get the whole opportunity, you can partner with a competitor and get a part of the opportunity.

Because information is now so readily available, one of way to help your company is by paying attention to competitors' product and service lines and serving as the conduit for information to others in your company.

* Are they making changes in pricing because the components are less expensive than they once were?
* Do they have better contracts with their suppliers than your company does?
* Are they marketing new product lines in new markets?
* Are they investing more money for research and development?

* Are they getting their new products and services to the market more quickly?

It's also vital for you to pay attention to what the customers are saying.

* What product and service innovations will your customers soon be asking for?
* What are they saying about your competition?

Internal Company Awareness

Most salespeople know they have to know everything about their customers—they delve into the information and don't take what they see at face value. Yet these same salespeople make assumptions about their own organizations.

It is important to face the facts, to really know and accept what is true about your own place of business. This means going beyond what the marketing materials tell you.

You know exactly what your company does well and what it doesn't. You can probably also tell what the likelihood is that you will have a client problem over the next month due to internal weakness.

If what you learn about your client's needs makes it clear that your company will not be able to deliver for reasons of timeliness or quality, you have an obligation to inform both the client *and* your management.

If you've done your homework and know your competition, you'll know if your competitors can meet their needs. Be the hero—make the referral. The customer is likely to come back to you in the future because you were honest with him. You've just become his champion and ally with a consultative sale because you are now the industry expert, not just a salesperson.

GUIDEPOST 23:

Research and stay on top of changes in your industry and in your competitors' businesses.

It is a sad fact that not all companies train the their salespeople well. Your customers assume you are fully trained on your company's product or service—meaning you know the features, the benefits, how it works, what industry it serves, and who the target market is, and that you know your company well enough to ethically stand behind the sale.

But as you and I both know, the truth is that a company's management will often not allocate the time and money to train salespeople at any more than a superficial level. A trained salesperson should be able to answer:

- Why did we create a particular product?
- What was the original intent?
- Who was the intended target audience?
- How confident are we that the product works?
- Are there flaws we already know about?
- What is the plan to create new products for next year or five years from now?

Sometimes the training is over after the initial hiring interview. "Oh, I see you've sold this kind of product before at another company. Great! You're hired—get out and sell."

Even if a salesperson is trained initially, industries change constantly. Unless there is intentional and continual training, simply keeping up with the changes is tough.

In technical fields, it is the rare person who understands the technical side and can relay that message to the non-technical customer. There is an expected disconnect for the foreseeable future, as there are neither enough technical people who are capable of selling nor people who know all the technology.

Even lower in priority on the training list is sales skill training. This is a disaster for the person new to sales who may have good instincts, but may be lacking a process. It's also a disservice to the experienced salesperson who knows the value of professional development.

PROOF POSITIVE

One of my first jobs as a salesperson was in a computer hardware business. Through a lot of persistence, I'd gotten to know the director of strategy for a major player in the industry at that time. This company was involved in a large project, and I was selling semiconductors and connectors. It was one of my first opportunities to make a big sale, and I was excited and proud to have gotten so far, so quickly.

I attended a meeting of about five of the company VIPs. They gave me all the information I needed to go back to my office, work with my management, and put together a great solution.

When it was time to present, I went through the specs, ending with an emphatic "This is the only solution for your issue. This is exactly what you need."

The same VIPs I had met initially sat around a table, politely finishing our conversation, but I knew something had just shifted. There was a definite chill in the air; something had gone wrong.

We shook hands at the end of the meeting, and my key contact (my champion) leaned over and said, "Deb, can I talk to you on the way to the car?"

When we got outside, he said, "Today I'm going to help you with a lesson that I hope you never forget while you're in business because I care about you, and I've seen how hard you work and I recognize the quality of your work."

He had my attention. I swallowed my pride and opened my ears.

"When you came in today, you had five people around that table, but the only person you really knew was me. I never dreamed you would walk back in here to present a single solution and then insist that it was the right solution. I expected you would come back with various scenarios. It seems everyone else in the room was at what we hope is the beginning of this sales relationship with you, and you were at the end."

He continued, "I'm telling you today you're not going to get this sale. I want you to redo your proposal the way it should have been done and come back to present it again. Shame on your management for not having properly prepared you. Given your potential and the potential of your company, this meeting could lead to a substantial increase in the revenue of your company."

Even if your company is like mine was and is not willing to invest in training, there is still no excuse for you to not find other ways to learn—talking to others as this man was willing to do for me, reading, taking classes—whatever it takes.

Self-awareness

The fourth type of knowledge you bring your company is self-awareness. Of course you must spend time getting to know your clients, your products, your business, and your industry, but the biggest blind spot we all have is awareness of ourselves.

Just knowing and accepting what you do well and what you don't do well is one of the most valuable qualities you can have. Knowing your own working style and what really hits your emotional buttons is a benefit when working through issues that are an inevitable part of the sales process.

GUIDEPOST 24:
Be self-aware—know what you and your company do well and what you don't.

A vital part of partnering with the people, both inside and outside your company, is leveraging everyone's strengths to minimize weaknesses across the board. If you do what you're best at, and everyone else does the same, the rest falls in line.

FIELD STUDIES

Consider performing market research to enhance your awareness. How could you use focus groups, mystery shoppers, or other activities to help build a better understanding of your customers and potential customers?

NEW TRAVELER TIPS

Create a call agenda of things you want to be aware of the next time you visit a client.

- What do you see when you walk into a client's place of business?
- What do you hear?
- What is the emotional climate?
- Are these happy people?
- Does management recognize employee achievement?
- Are there any signs of financial problems?

* Do employees seem active, productive, and engaged?
* Is the office neat and well-kept?
* Can you document what you see and give this information to other people in your office so you can all better plan for the next step in working with this client?

SEASONED CLIMBER CHALLENGE

Do you have a complete understanding of your business and your industry?

* What's true in your industry?
* What is the elephant in the room in your company that no one wants to talk about but is holding everyone back?
* What do your competitors do that makes a difference to your customers?
* Are you really prepared when you make a sales call? Do you know everything you need to know about your clients and your product?
* Have you invested in your own sales training and education? Have you kept up with the best tools of the trade?

ASK DEB

Q: When I am out in the marketplace, I always run into this guy from the competition. He promises the moon and I know he doesn't deliver. I have lost five orders to him in the last six months. I'm so frustrated, and I just want people to know he isn't all he appears to be. What should I do?

A: *First, remember one of our cardinal rules in selling: NEVER badmouth the competition.*

Next, remember you want to concentrate on the lifetime value of your client and not on just one or two orders. If you think in terms of doing business with these clients for the long term, it gives you time to figure out what to do and release the stress you are feeling right now.

If you know what the competitor is promising and not delivering, you want to craft your questions carefully before you go to your next sales call with your client. Remember to be careful not to ask yes/no questions; instead, ask open-ended questions that will allow you to get more information from the client so you can understand why he is buying from your competition. Think about who, what, where, when, why, how questions. Asking these types of questions can help the client articulate how he likes to work with suppliers, help you formulate a better approach for the next time, and keep you from losing sleep over having lost a piece of business to a turkey.

For example:

- *How was your experience when you bought this product last time?*

- *When you developed this product, how did you determine what the pricing should be?*

- *Why do you have only one source for this product?*

- *What do you like most about your current supplier? What would you like to be different?*

Want more help on your journey?

See www.TheFieldGuideToSales.com for the Awareness of the Environment Workbook

CREATIVITY WINS THE DAY

CHAPTER 9

In order to bend and break the rules, you must first understand them. Once you have prepared adequately, packed skillfully, and are confident in your survival skills, you won't hesitate to strike out off the beaten path to make the sale.

There is no limit to your income. There is no limit to the number of people you can serve, and there's no limit to the creative new possibilities that exist as long as you stay in that mindset.

Successful people are highly creative. They cultivate new ways of thinking and of being in the world. Creativity is critical to staying one step ahead of the competition, both in the products and services created and in the way they are presented.

Most people don't connect creativity with sales, but creativity is a big part of putting new approaches to real use in the marketplace.

As we've said throughout, what you are selling, first and foremost, is you. You are a unique individual, and the more you differentiate yourself, the more your own unique "brand" is valued. One of the most effective ways to differentiate is through creativity.

How can you, as a professional salesperson, keep it fresh day after day? Can you:

* Make it fun for the people around you and recognize the appropriate opportunities to do so?
* Continue to learn and seek new sources of ideas?
* Use your environment as a source of creativity?
* Get out of the office and into the world?

Put Some Madness in your Method

Each sales call must be about three things:

* Serving your customer
* Maximizing your revenue
* Creating a mutually profitable relationship

There is so much room for individual expression within each of these areas that the possibilities are limitless.

Each of us wants to enjoy what we do, and our customers are no different. Find new ways to give each of them great customer experiences, and they are yours for life. With each new company, each new individual, each new product line, comes another chance to erase the preconceived ideas. Any salesperson can deliver the product and pick up the check. Strive to be unique...strive to be unforgettable!

GUIDEPOST 25:
Creativity is essential to the development of the career salesperson.

Try to imagine yourself in your customers' shoes—what are their challenges? What really gets them up in the morning? Since you come to it with your own set of experiences, you can help them get a new perspective. Wouldn't it be wonderful to serve as your customers' source of creativity!

Some of the most gratifying business experiences we can have are when we are working with other people toward a common goal, and we work extra hard and extra long and we solve problems together by just throwing whatever we have out on the table to see if someone else can build on those ideas.

Consider the routine things you do with your customers—sending proposals, delivering samples, providing the product or service, sending them reports and invoices. What if any or all of these things could be done in a more fun or inventive way?

PROOF POSITIVE

I have a client in the food manufacturing business whose customers are restaurants. When a new restaurant opens, he puts a big bow on one case of each of the products he sells to the restaurant as a "welcome and good luck" gift and delivers it at the grand opening party...it's always a hit!

Do you write "thank you" on your invoices? Do you send thank-you notes or other cards? Send cards at occasions other than the winter holidays; for example, send "have a great vacation" postcards at the beginning of the summer, and tell your customers you will be working hard for them while they are gone and look forward to seeing them when they return. Make every day you work together an occasion to remember.

An Open Mind Opens Doors

Sales is, in some ways, an inherently creative pursuit. You visit new companies every day and brainstorm with new people to see how your products and services can be used creatively within their business processes to come up with something new and different to enhance productivity and profitability. No two companies you deal with are exactly alike and, of course, neither are their needs.

The problem is, as we get more and more experience and expertise in a profession, we start to feel like we've seen it all. It is harder and harder to stay open to new ideas. It gets easier just to do it the way we've always done it, because it has always worked that way.

That may be true, but it isn't much fun for you or your clients.

GUIDEPOST 26:
Stay open, creative, and learning.

Regimented sales training tends to teach a rote process that discourages people from veering too far from it. While training in the sales process is important, we need to train ourselves to think outside the box as well.

Attend sales conferences and training sessions where only creativity is on the agenda!

We live in a time where we can instantly access almost anything we want to. The opportunity to listen to creative geniuses in every field (*including sales*) is as close as your computer or MP3 player.

Take risks in expressing yourself authentically. You can't be afraid you aren't creative or that your ideas aren't good enough. Those are creativity killers.

Get in the habit of writing down your creative lightning strikes as soon as you have them. Keep a creativity journal or a file of those ideas, and refer to it often.

Energize Your Environment

Why is the shower a common birthplace for creative thought? There are several reasons—you are busy with something that doesn't take any thought, freeing your mind to wander. There is white noise, the water, that helps your brain go inside instead of listening for outside noise, and finally, you have changed your environment.

How odd and unfortunate that our offices, and most of the rooms of our homes, are not nearly as conducive to creative thought as our showers.

Changing your viewpoint can make you look at everything in a whole new way, so shift the position of your desk, put toys within reach and keep a bulletin board of funny, creative pictures and sayings.

Once your creative juices are flowing, look for ways to express that new creativity to prospects and clients with your own blog, newsletters, or articles.

The next time you think of sending something to a customer, make it something you think might enhance creativity for them.

PROOF POSITIVE

I had a meeting with a new prospect over breakfast a number of years ago, and as soon as I got back to the office, I sat down to write a note thanking the gentleman for his time.

Without thinking, I put a happy face next to my signature, something I'd done routinely on personal notes to close friends.

Oh, I thought, I can't send that out to a prospect; I have to rewrite the note before I send it without the happy face. Then I thought again and decided to take a chance and mail it as is.

When he received the note, the prospect called. Although we didn't know each other well, instead of saying hello and identifying himself, he said, "Deb, no one has ever sent me a note with a happy face on it before."

It took me a moment to realize who it was, but as soon as I did, I burst out laughing and so did he. Then he said, "Obviously, I need to know you better. Can I buy you lunch?"

That was the start of a great business relationship that continues to this day. Although we've had many more serious conversations than light ones over the course of creating lucrative business deals for us both, he still tells the story of the happy face on the note as the reason for our connection.

The World is Your Oyster

Here's a good reason to stay current and creative: So many people do what they do and never change. The world around them changes, but they stay put. One day they wake up and they're no longer engaged, or even relevant. Their style doesn't work. Their methodologies don't work. They are stuck. Take advantage of all the world has to offer—don't let it pass you by. Grab your pearl from that oyster.

GUIDEPOST 27:
Enjoy the world of opportunities you uniquely have as a professional salesperson.

Sales is an uncommonly portable skill and is used in every part of the world. So if you aren't happy doing what you are doing, maybe you are selling the wrong things or selling in the wrong place. Maybe you can use your skills in a whole new way.

I've found some of the most creative people in sales combine two things in unique ways. The salesperson with technical or creative expertise can do amazing things. If your passions include sports, or architecture or music, then find ways to sell within these communities or to use these passions in your sales processes.

Sometimes we demonstrate who we are and what we do in the most powerful way outside the work environment by doing things that are meaningful to our hearts, not our wallets. Invite your prospects or clients to join you for a project you are passionate about, like building houses for Habitat for Humanity. Or better yet, volunteer to help with an organization that is meaningful to your client.

Imagine the impression you leave if, for no money-motivated reason, you regularly show up and give of your time and expertise. You build natural relationships, and they see you working in a collaborative way. They get to take your measure in a no-pressure environment, and they'll take this impression back to the office with them.

When they come to know you as bright, inventive, fun, and a great collaborator, why would they think of doing business with anyone else? People want to do business with people they know, like, trust, and feel they connect with.

FIELD STUDIES

Consider how to use these readily available creativity resources:

* TV—You're watching it anyway, so pay a little closer attention to what catches your interest and why.

* Books—There are many volumes on creative subjects. Pick three that seem weird to you and read them with an open mind for new ideas.
* Magazines—Stand in front of a bookstore's magazine rack and look at magazines you aren't familiar with. Look at them, read them, study them.
* Starbucks—Sales meetings take place all the time over coffee. Eavesdrop (discreetly).
* Internet—Cultivate a list of websites and blogs that inspire your inner creative genius and access them regularly.

NEW TRAVELER TIPS

Ask others for creative ideas they have used with their customers. This will be the beginning of your creative list. Pay attention to what others do, and update your list frequently. Remember to look for ideas in all industries, not just your own.

SEASONED CLIMBER CHALLENGE

Do you have clients who work in industries you find fascinating? Go to their industry conferences to learn more about the industries you serve, how they think, and what their upcoming challenges are. Can you connect their challenges to your sales process?

ASK DEB

Q: How do I use creativity to get clients to try my products when price and budget is a major factor?

A: *Offer customers a pertinent sample or demonstration. Be sure your packaging or presentation effectively show the product's solution to the client's need or problem in a memorable way.*

For example, a technology called stereo lithography allows you to create a model of a product from a computer drawing. Motorola used this technology to create a model of a phone that would fit into a man's shirt pocket when they first presented the concept of a phone that could be taken anywhere. Imagine going into the meeting without a presentation, per se, but with this model of a concept and just setting it out on the table and asking people to pick it up, put it in their pocket, see how light it felt. Think of how people who were carrying around cell phones the size of a brick felt when they first picked up a small phone. Who wouldn't want one of those? This was creative genius.

Price and budget are always a factor, but what you want to establish is that your products solve the customer's need or problem.

If you first establish the need, the customer will begin to believe you can deliver the solution, that your company is easy to do business with, and he can have a great relationship with you. This way, price will not be the number one thing they are using to decide, even though that might be what they start out saying.

Also, if you think budget is an issue with a client, be sure to ask qualifying questions up front before you get too far along in the process. If you determine there really is no budget this quarter, this year, or whatever, it doesn't make sense to have discussions about value and price in the first place!

Being creative can get prospects' attention, and they might buy quicker than you ever imagined...even if they thought they didn't have a budget.

Brilliant ideas have been known to "create" budgets where they once were thought not to exist...how many people do you know who have tiny cell phones that fit in their pockets today?

Want more help on your journey?

See www.TheFieldGuideToSales.com for the Creativity Wins the Day Workbook

GETTING WHAT YOU CAME FOR

CHAPTER 10

Congratulations. You've reached the top and you're halfway there! Yes, halfway. You didn't think this was the end, did you? Make no mistake; heading skillfully down the mountain is as important and challenging as climbing up.

When the time is right, you will ask for the sale. Yes, ask. If you don't ask for it, you won't get it. But if you ask for it before the customer is ready to give it to you, you won't get it, either.

The customer isn't thinking about you and whether you should or should not get an order. He's thinking about investing in something that changes his business. He's trying to decide if this is a big gamble, something he's relatively unsure of, or if this is a sure thing—a reasonable investment for the possible or probable benefit to his business. Once he has arrived at the conclusion you've been leading him to, ask for the sale.

PROOF POSITIVE

A great salesperson for a major restaurant supply firm makes the point this way: He doesn't sell food to restaurants. He sells restaurants on his company's inventory system and how the food moves through that system to client restaurants.

They aren't just selling steaks, chicken, and vegetables, so they aren't competing with other food sellers. And they continue to grow that system to be more information-rich and more useful to the customer. So the firm will never be confused with commodity sellers.

What do many of his prospects expect before the first sales call? They expect to get his price list so they can compare it to the other top-quality vendors and make a decision on price.

But when he shows up, they find themselves talking about how they want to lower inventory and free up cash, how they want more deliveries of smaller quantities, and all the things the right system could help them manage. Do you think they will be buying food from this guy? Food, and a whole lot more.

If you and your customers haven't been having open, back-and-forth conversations about their problems, it's highly unlikely anyone will be buying your solution.

Don't Slip and Fall

When you think about asking for the sale, when you imagine in your mind sitting in front of your prospect and saying whatever you say to close the sale, think about these things:

* What are you trying to accomplish here?
* Who are you on the planet?
* Who are you in your company?
* Who are you in front of this prospect?
* Are you genuinely coming from a place of service?
* Is this sale something you will feel good about in a week or a year from now?

If you don't care about people and you don't care about the client, and you just want to get this order because you have bills to pay, then whatever technique you use to close the sale will be just fine.

It is relatively easy to teach people words to use so people can't say no, even if they have good reasons to want to.

Remember the old life insurance tactic of having the wife in the room and asking the husband, "Don't you want them to have everything if you aren't here to provide it?" You couldn't say no to that question without putting your marriage at risk, regardless of whether insurance was the best thing for your family.

This is a forcing type close, where the victim feels pressured to buy versus a close that flows to the natural conclusion that being secure in the future is possible with these insurance products today.

GUIDEPOST 28:
The close is just one step in the middle of a long sales relationship process.

Before you have asked for the order, here's what the customer is considering:

* How much better would my world be with this product or service?

* Can I trust the person in front of me enough to believe he and his company are capable of delivering what we need, when we need it?"

If you have done you job well the customer will likely give clues or share with you, to some degree, why the possibility of working with you appeals to him. At that point, you are ready to take the order.

Anyone who has taken sales training courses knows that a substantial amount of time is always devoted to "the close." There are any number of typical approaches, but I quit using them a long time ago. They all boil down to a manipulation—saying something so the customer feels he or she can't say no.

This might be fine for a one-time sale, but making your customer feel pushed into something is not a very effective relationship-building technique.

You can use techniques all day long, but if you're coming from other than a place of service, then these approaches will all be ineffective at maintaining the lifetime value of the customer.

So What Brings You Here?

There is another aspect to the sales process that isn't discussed very often: Do you and your company want to make this sale? Is this going to be a profitable relationship for you?

The lure of the sales profession is its potential to make lots and lots of money. But there is another incentive that can be just as intoxicating to people in sales, and that is the prestige of winning. Sales people generally love winning awards and being recognized.

Owners of thoroughbred horses don't enter the Kentucky Derby for the purse as much as for the considerable prestige of winning.

Sales compensation often includes incentives, commissions, perks, and benefits—all used to motivate and inspire the salesperson to sell more.

Which brings us to an important point: Just because you can get a sale, should you? Even if you are standing at the summit, about to watch the client sign on the dotted line, it's not too late to stop a disaster from happening. If you are only in it for the thrill of closing the deal, take a step back and think carefully about whether or not this deal is a fit for you and your company.

This moment is what I was referring at the beginning of this chapter when I pointed out that going down is as challenging as climbing up. If you have made a "good" sale that is a fit, you don't have to worry. You still have to follow up and stay on top of things, but it will be a pleasant task. If you have made a "bad" sale, the trip downhill, through production, delivery, and beyond, will be arduous. Choose your deals wisely.

PROOF POSITIVE

> I recently ran into someone I had mentored the previous year. We exchanged pleasantries, and I asked her how things were going. Jumping out at me from her account of current clients was one that simply didn't make sense to me based on what she sold and what that company might buy.
>
> "Yes," she sighed, "you warned me about trying to fit square pegs into round holes, and you were right. I worked so hard to get that sale, and it has been twice as much work as any of my other clients ever since. It's a giant albatross around my neck."

GUIDEPOST 29:
Ask only for sales that will be profitable and manageable for you and for the company.

One way to gauge whether you are about to make a good or a bad sale, other than trusting your gut and looking at all the information you've gathered, is to look at your own commission structure.

Company objectives and the compensation structure for the salesperson, which is usually part commission or incentive, must align. One critical measurement is total sales dollars, but another key measurement is *profitable* sales dollars. If the sales dollars coming in are equal to the money the company expends in the transaction, then the sale might as well not have come in at all.

Another measurement often used in incentive programs is the measurement of the increase in sales compared to the same time last year. So, if you did 10 million in sales last year and you do 12 million in sales the next year, there will be an extra incentive for having increased that business.

Sometimes there are additional incentives for customer retention or repeat business. The most profitable sales are usually from repeat customers, so there may be a good reason to create an incentive to make those sales rather than sales from new customers.

The company and the salespeople must be working from the same playbook, and on the same time frame. The executive team may be really focused on a five-year plan. Even if the executives' compensation is based on a five-year plan, sales compensation is based on a one-year plan—at most. But there still may be tie-ins to the five-year plan to make sure new customers fit the profile of where the executives would like the company to be in five years.

Persistence = Payoff

According to the Laboratory of Advertising Performance, a division of McGraw Hill Research, the following is true of a salesperson for each prospect they attempt to connect with:

* Forty-eight percent of all sales people call a prospect only once.
* Twenty-five percent quit after the second call.
* Ten percent of all salespeople keep calling until they have a final yes or no.
* Eighty percent of sales are made after five or more calls.

Interesting that making the sale seems more dependent on the persistence of the salesperson than the close he uses.

Once you are certain this is the right relationship for your company, and you are equally certain this is the right investment for your client, then you can gracefully guide this continuing conversation to the next phase of your relationship, which may include money, contract, and delivery of products and services.

If you make large sales and relatively few per year close because of the nature of the sales cycle in your industry, then you need ways to keep all your sales skills sharp.

GUIDEPOST 30:
Keep your sales skills sharp

Taking continuing training sessions, working with a coach, or taking on a variety of sales challenges—some short-term, some longer, are all ways of keeping your skills honed.

The only difference between Sales 101 and a Ph.D. in sales is practice. The more opportunity you have to challenge your skills in real or close-to-real sales situations, the better you will become at recognizing customer signals of objections and the other signals that say they are ready to get going.

You actually practice closing every day. You may not get the order every day, but you close on something—you close when you get the meeting, or the referral, or the information you need to take the interaction to the next step.

Professional salespeople always have a fallback position. So if they don't take the order, they make an appointment for a follow-up conversation to get an answer to the customer's concerns.

There are many steps before the close and many steps after. We seem to have imposed a distinction that doesn't serve us well; that everything prior to asking for the sale is one sort of process and asking for the sale is something very different.

Getting to a close is also perceived as a big hurdle to get over, and if you don't do it yesterday and do it right, the rest of your work and relationship-building is for naught.

Talk about a confidence and motivation killer! Salespeople are often so anxious about the process and so focused on the close that they are unable to absorb what the customer is saying and be open to the responses they are getting.

No one (except you) cares about the number of no's you get, but they do care about the yeses. You may need to hear a large number of no's to get to the yeses, so get going!

The Other Side of the Mountain

Are you in this just for the money, or in it to help the customer? That is going to become very obvious with what you do right after the close and after the money has changed hands. Do you leave the scene and get right on to your next conquest, leaving any problems to customer service?

I hope not, because what he does next it is a measure of a salesperson's intent and character. You continue to represent the company to that client. Any salesperson worth his salt will make sure the product or service delivery is handled fully and well.

If it is your company's policy to have customer service or other tech people take over the account at this point, it is your responsibility to make a graceful handoff.

Much as a parent's relationship with his children changes as they become adults, you will always, we hope, have an important relationship with this client, even if it changes as the client works more directly with other people at your company.

FIELD STUDIES

Define other areas in your life where you have no problem asking for what you want. What's different about those areas that you can apply to how you think about selling?

NEW TRAVELER TIPS

Create a checklist for the close that works for you and your sales process. What things must be accomplished before you are ready to ask for the order? What language and expressions are you looking for to get the sense that the customer is ready to buy?

SEASONED CLIMBER CHALLENGE

Challenge yourself with these questions:

* What is your batting average? How many yeses do you get for each no?
* Has it improved over the past year? If not, what can you do about that?
* Do you spend any time mentoring or teaching other salespeople?
* Do you practice by teaching or in any other way?
* Do you have someone you can call on to help you with your most challenging sales situations? Do you call them when you need help, or do you tough it out alone?
* Do you have a sales coach?

ASK DEB

Q: How do I get over my fear of hearing no? I'm afraid to ask for the sale.

A: *"NO" can be like a nagging headache, so take a couple of Tylenol and it will go away pretty soon.*

If a client says "no" today, they are simply saying they can't say "yes" today.

The best way to get over fear of rejection is simply to decide: "Today I am going to ask for the order!" The decision is the first step, and often the biggest. If you will ask for the order, not all the answers you get will be NO … some will be YES. Think of NO as a stepping-stone to YES.

Prepare by establishing a process you will use when you do hear no. Review the situation: Why did you get a "no" today? Do they have questions that haven't been fully answered? Were you missing something in your understanding of their needs? Did you not clearly articulate to them the value of your product or service in solving their problem?

Whatever you do, never let a "NO" stop you from continuing to move forward, whether it is to move forward to get a different result or to move forward and continue on your way to finding another client/customer that will be a better fit for you and your company.

Want more help on your journey?

See www.TheFieldGuideToSales.com for the Getting What You Came For Workbook

OVERCOMING OBSTACLES

CHAPTER 11

Sometimes your adventure will come to a halt when the trail ends suddenly. Sometimes it will fizzle out slowly as you determine you just can't take another step. But you'll have to figure out a way to keep moving forward. How you do that will have a huge bearing on your long-term career success.

The sales process can be a winding trek. It's a long way to "yes," and there are many, many rocks in the road to get around before you get there.

How do you keep smiling and keep going? How do you keep from getting short with the customers and your co-workers? How do you treat yourself well when you wonder if this is the right job, product, or career for you?

When the Best-laid Plans Fall Short

There is a lot of opportunity to practice dealing with rejection in sales. Maybe you can't even get in the door. Maybe the receptionist won't tell you who handles the purchasing of your product in her company. Maybe the decision-maker was a no-show for your appointment. Or maybe you got the definitive "no"—they just aren't willing to do business with your company.

There are few careers that test your character and resolve like sales. And the big lessons all come out of business you lose.

GUIDEPOST 31:
The feedback you get from a "no" may be more valuable to you than a "YES, you got the sale."

Does rejection debilitate you so you can't move forward? Do you take it personally, feeling as though you are defending yourself? If you keep looking at it this way, it is going to be a long road to sales success.

There are always going to be objections. You will never live in the sales world where, one after another, people buy without question. If you do find yourself in that environment, expect to be replaced shortly by a clerk who takes orders and fills them, no sales involved.

And, as much as you may think you are in control, you are not. There will always be reasons you can't know as to why you might not get a sale. Spend time deconstructing what happened, attempt to learn from it, and then let it go.

Show Your True Colors

Handling objections is part of the sales job, but it can get tedious and tiresome. Some prospects are just never satisfied!

How do you handle legitimate questions from your customers? Do you think of them as objections, roadblocks to get over, around, or through? Are they just a part of doing whatever it takes? Do you think of it as taking one for the team?

An objection is a sign that there is some point of fear or concern on the part of the client that you haven't yet addressed or realized.

GUIDEPOST 32:
Objections are part of the sales process. How you handle them may be what the customer wants to know.

One of the first statements I make when I conduct sales trainings is that you should never, ever lie. And more often than not, I will have some brave soul stop me and say, "but everybody does it."

I respond by pointing out the error in that perception. I don't lie to prospects and customers, so I know that not all salespeople do it. If you want to be in the top 10 percent of salespeople, then you won't lie, either. The best salespeople retain their customers, and those customers refer others. If a salesperson lies to his current customers, he will constantly be replacing them, not adding to them.

The reason we lie is to save face or because we aren't happy with the facts. But the truth is the truth. The delivery date is the delivery date, the price is the price, and the quality is the quality. You can lie, stretch the truth, cover up, and divert attention, but only for so long. Eventually, the truth will come out.

We struggle because our egos make it hard for us to face what we perceive to be failure and rejection. We want to be the conquering heroes, even if the company can't handle the business in the competitive market.

More salespeople lie by omission than by saying something that isn't true. They just hope the customer won't think to ask until the money is on their side of the table.

Start dealing only with the truth. You'll find you sleep better at night, and your customers will respond more favorably.

Getting Tired and Cranky?

Is this you?

* Do you get easily frustrated?
* Do things have to be under your control in order for you to be happy?
* Do you feel your blood pressure rising when you face an objection? Is your first reaction to start talking and defending?

If so, sales is going to be tough for you.

Remember, sales is about the relationship. Listen to objections. In fact, lean in and listen even more intently. The number one reason for an objection is the customer doesn't feel heard—that you don't really understand where he is coming from. Remain calm—do not get defensive.

Learn from what you hear so you can use that knowledge to be motivated enough to get out there and try, try again.

Sometimes your biggest frustrations are with yourself, or with having to live with the reality that you have done something to adversely impact an opportunity. Despite your protests, maybe the reason you didn't get the order is because *you* didn't follow up on time. Did you promise that the order could be delivered on Tuesday, knowing full well that the earliest delivery date possible was Thursday?

PROOF POSITIVE

If you want a view of what it looks like from the outside when you don't handle frustration well, observe young children when the natural consequences of their actions find them faced with less than desirable outcomes. The blow to the ego results in crying and shouting tantrums, manipulating to get what they want, and blaming other people. The adult version is just as unpleasant.

I had a client who telephoned me screaming the moment anything seemed to be wrong, even before he had checked to verify the problem. After the third episode, I told him I didn't think I was a good match for his business and offered to help him place his business elsewhere. Stunned, he told me how much he enjoyed working with me and how much he appreciated my responsiveness to his concerns. I told him that most of the time I enjoyed him, too, but that shouting and cursing were things I had long ago decided I didn't want in my life. He apologized and has never done that again. I'm not suggesting he hasn't continued that behavior with others in his life, but he knows that isn't the best way to work with me.

How you react to disappointment will tell your clients a lot more about you than anything else. If you gracefully talk to them after the loss of the contract and keep in touch, you never know what may happen next. If the contract with the awarded vendor doesn't go well—and we all know that is entirely possible—you might have a second chance at the contract.

The additional respect you build when you've lost a contract is worth a fortune. That, alone, could be the reason you win next time. Don't forget that buyers often move between companies, and they will remember how you performed for their past employers as well.

One of the biggest frustrations for the salesperson is when the decision is made on a political basis or when the decision was made even before the prospect contacted you. Perhaps you were brought in for due diligence (sometimes a prospect needs three bids to meet company policies or government regulations) or to help the customer negotiate a better price with their current supplier.

Your hope, in doing relationship-building work, is that the prospect will level with you and will be willing to include you as a "legitimate" player later in exchange for your help with the current situation.

You have a right to be frustrated, disappointed, and even angry. But what you do with it is the difference between the amateur and the pro.

Try, Try Again

I think it is reasonable for a salesperson who has expended a lot of time, energy, and company money over the course of weeks or months in meetings and in following up, researching solutions, and creating proposals, to ask the question, "What could I have done differently?"

You owe it to yourself and to your company to see if you can get an answer.

Bear in mind, the customer is likely to give you an objection that leaves both of you with your dignity. Even if the reason for the "no" was that she didn't like you, she is likely to talk about price or in some other way to make this seem like a logical, objective decision.

Hopefully, if you convey how important their candor is to you for your own self-development efforts, you might get more of the story. If you do get to the real reason, the value of that feedback may be greater to you than the money you might have gotten from the sale.

It is important to do a post mortem on every sales opportunity, win or lose, alone, with your boss, and perhaps with your sales coach.

Earn the right to be taken seriously.

Unlikely Opportunities

It is not that unusual for a customer to be worried or disappointed. It may be buyer's remorse, or worry over whether it was a good choice—even before the product is delivered.

Sometimes, after the sale, customers are disappointed with the quality of the product or service, and on a human level, they are disappointed with you. They trusted your opinion that they needed the product or service, that your company could deliver it, and that it would solve their problems. That opinion has been tested; as a result, the customer has lost confidence in you. You may have to re-establish that trust in your relationship, demonstrating that you are still committed to what you are delivering and to what they are expecting.

The stereotype of salespeople in the general public is that they'll say anything to get the deal. Those salespeople give us all a bad name. But if you ever err on the side of wishful thinking rather than on what you know you can deliver, you can expect to deal with problems after the sale.

GUIDEPOST 33:
Be straightforward and committed to the deal, especially AFTER it's done.

Life in the Trenches

The sales process is not as much fun as it seems to the outside world. It isn't all about business trips, nice restaurants, and golf. Most of the time, it is about calling, and calling and calling again. It requires doing research and writing up expense reports. And we don't have the luxury of as much administrative help as we used to. Most of us are doing our own prospecting and follow-up letters and emails.

Some salespeople consider themselves above the process and above doing what it takes. These are the ones who won't deliver samples

OVERCOMING OBSTACLES 163

themselves and won't go out of their way to provide service once the deal is done.

Like any career, sales has its ups and downs—great days and days that we just can't get it right.

But for those of us who do it and love it, we are willing to take the good days and the bad, just to get to those great days when we know we've made connections that will last a lifetime and when we've made a lasting difference in our clients' businesses and their lives.

FIELD STUDIES

Talk to salespeople in other industries about their sales process. Do they make cold calls? How many calls do they make to turn a prospect into a customer? What is the lead time to make a sale? Bring sales techniques that work in other industries to yours.

NEW TRAVELER TIPS

List all the objections you have ever heard from a prospect or customer about your product or service. Now list the answers (the honest answers) to each objection. Use the list as a reference tool for future sales opportunities.

List the most common problems you see after the sale. Did you build any expectations that you know aren't realistic for what you and your company can deliver? How can you be loyal, optimistic, and honest at the same time?

SEASONED CLIMBER CHALLENGE

See if you can weather these questions:

* Be honest with yourself: What is the one lie you find yourself telling your prospects or clients? What do you hope to avoid by telling this lie?

* What was your most frustrating or disappointing sales experience? What did you learn from it?

* What have you learned from your mentors and coaches, or by watching other salespeople? What differentiates the pros from the amateurs?

* Why are you in sales? What do you love? What is the hardest part for you?

ASK DEB

Q: Price is the single most important part in auto sales. How do you overcome price objections?

A: *So, you believe that price is the single most important part in auto sales?*

Not knowing how many cars you have sold in your lifetime, could you maybe think of just the last ten cars you sold? After the sale, did you ask why the individual bought the car from you? If so, did each buyer tell you he bought because of the price? Or was it something else? Was your dealership the only one who had the car he wanted in stock? Or were you were so easy to deal with and helpful that he decided to buy from you? Or did he buy from you because of the service your dealership offers after the sale? Or were you geographically desirable?

If price is the only objection someone has to buying from you and everything comes down to price, why don't you begin the next discussion with someone who wants to buy a car with talking about price? Most often people who sell cars talk about everything else — the model, the features, the ride, the feel, the benefits, the gas mileage, even the color — before they talk about price. But if price is the most important thing, why wait until last to talk about it?

Next time a customer comes to your dealership, spend a little time making a connection, and then ask what make and model he is interested in. Then ask what price range he has in mind.

You want to sell as many cars as possible in the shortest time possible, and he wants to buy a car easily and affordably. Getting to the information you want to know more quickly can help him

THE FIELD GUIDE TO SALES

get the answer he needs more quickly, which is whether he can afford the car.

Do you really want to talk to someone who wants a particular vehicle but has no way to pay for it? Maybe you do, because while they can't buy today, they may be able to in the future. Or maybe you don't want to talk to him because your experience says if they don't buy today, they won't be back.

If price is truly the main consideration, if this really is just a commodity, then you might as well be direct with them up front and ask what price range they are looking for so you can get on to working with other customers if you can't help this one.

Want more help on your journey?

See www.TheFieldGuideToSales.com for the Overcoming Obstacles Workbook

JUST DO IT

CHAPTER 12

My goal with this book is to bring your focus to, or back to, the time-tested fundamentals of the sales process. The five biggest mistakes made by salespeople go back to not applying the fundamentals:

1. They don't quantify and qualify the customers they really want and what they need for their business to thrive.
2. They aren't prepared to make the first call.
3. They don't make a second, third, or fourth call.
4. They don't ask open-ended questions and don't stop talking long enough to hear the customer.
5. They see objections, not opportunities.

Do you see any of your habits on that list? If so, start making changes today. Even making a small improvement will bring big results in the months to come.

Just do it. Take action to change just one of these dynamics, and you'll see the sales adventure become a lot more fun and profitable. You don't have to be great to get started, but you do have to get started to be great.

Some of the most effective proactive habits for sales people include:

* Developing and following a plan to develop new suspects every day without fail.
* Following up and take the next steps with all prospects and leads, quickly and effectively.
* Actively intervene to take care of customer problems as soon as you know about them.

You can have the best intentions in the world, but without a commitment to daily, weekly, and monthly action, intentions become wishes, with little hope of coming true.

Make yourself accountable to someone, even if that someone is you (and you will need the discipline of a Marine).

The basics are the same for everyone. Continue to improve your sales skills and push yourself out of your comfort zone—just a little. Make one more phone call, use a different sales tool, push yourself to exceed your weekly goal. Every step you take toward growing your sales repertoire makes what you've just learned easier. Each skill builds upon the previous one.

Sales success comes from focusing on making your sales efforts better and more effective. It's also about enjoying the process of sales. Working through each phase of the sales process will make your sales activities more enjoyable. You'll know what your goals are, and you'll have the tools to help you meet those goals. You will continue to increase those goals. No matter where you are on the sales continuum, using a proven process will make the sales process easier and more profitable than you can imagine!

Are you the type of person who absolutely hates sales and believes you can't sell? Or the type who buys all the latest sales books yet hardly cracks the spine on any of them? Or do you take on sales with the vigor of an Olympic athlete?

If there's anything I would like for you to leave with, it is the idea that you CAN sell and, if you don't give up, you will accomplish your sales goals. Be honest with yourself, do your best, and it will come. Accept that there will be ups and downs on the way to the finish line.

I hope when you are struggling with a difficult call, client or situation, you will take out this book and reacquaint yourself with the things you already know. They are fundamental to the successful sale every time. There is no secret to selling; it is a process. You hold in your hand the *Field Guide To Sales* to lead you through the process. So get out there and SELL—no excuses!!

Want more help on your journey?
See www.TheFieldGuideToSales.com for the Just Do It Workbook

ACKNOWLEDGMENTS

Kym "YOU NEED A BOOK PERIOD. Now, let's get going!" Yancey
www.eWomenNetwork.com

Jan "Publishing A Book Is Possible!" King
www.eWomenPublishingNetwork.com

Tina Ferguson, Queen of Dreams That Come True
www.TinaFerguson.com

THE COACH for Success Steve Straus
www.StrausUSA.com

Wordsmith Maria Smith makes your words sound good on paper.
www.thewordsmithgroup.com

Dawn Putney Book Design Artist Extraordinaire
www.ToolboxCreative.com

Genius-Creative-Fun Gail Richards
www.authorsmart.com

Chief Strategist and Map Maker Anu Venkitaraman
www.ReThinkMarketing.com

Public Relations Field Scout Roy Miller
www.RGMcomms.com

Budding Brain Surgeon and Camp Mrazek Coordinator Shawn Nguyen
www.nejm.org (ok, so she isn't there yet, but she will be!)

Those who kept the embers hot on the campfire

Gayle Golladay,
Reggie Harvey,
Nancy Barry,
www.NancyBarry.com
Stu Schlackman,
www.Competitive-Excellence.com,
Kim Duke,
www.SalesDivas.com

...and the extra s'mores go to my All-Time favorite Mrazek campers—Tommy, Jason, Jennifer, Happy, Hailey Mary, and Season... without them there would be no meaning and fun in this great adventure called LIFE.

For all of you who have participated in my wild and exhilarating adventures in one way or another—thank you!! :)

ABOUT THE AUTHOR

Business people and salespersons across the United States call her a sales coach. Her clients call her a Godsend.

Debbie Mrazek is a doer and dynamo who delivers a sales prescription that really works. Whether you're a novice or expert at selling products or services, Mrazek's sales mantra and methods resonate a clear, complete picture for certain success.

Mrazek is founder and president of The Sales Company, a Texas-based firm that is helping hundreds of entrepreneurs, individuals, and large corporations better assess, understand, and engage in practical, purposeful selling.

With "Mrazek Energy" (believed to be from another world since it is a constant flow of happiness and enthusiasm), Debbie teaches the tools, techniques, and talents every individual possesses, and how to transform those into s-a-l-e-s. Mrazek has counseled, constructed, and completed sales programs, workshops, and individual and team coaching across the nation. She's also a speaker, author, and conference facilitator.

When she's not out helping the world improve their sales, Mrazek enjoys life's adventures with husband Tommy, son Jason, daughter Jennifer, two beagles Happy and Hailey Mary, and lazy calico cat Season.

www.TheFieldGuideToSales.com
www.The-Sales-Company.com

INDEX

#

80-20 rule, 18

A

account profiles, 67
active listening, 105–108
appointments, confirming, 45
attitude, preparing, 52
awareness
    of client's situation, 118–121
    internal company, 123–126
    of industry and competitors, 122–123

SELF-, 126–127

B

bad prospects, 96–97, 149
body language, 94
buyer's remorse, 163

C

call agenda, 127–128
champion inside company, 49–50

clients,
    relationships with, 161–162
    researching clients, 43
    unspoken communications of, 45, 51
coach, sales 82–83
cold calling, fear of, 30
communication
    bad prospects, deterring, 96–97
    body language, 94
    of disconnects, 73, 74
client, 90-91, 110
    listeners, types of, 108–109
    listening-talking ratio, 111
    messages to prospect, 92–94
    questions, asking open-ended 92
    silence, 105
    venue for meeting, 110
    within company, 97
compensation, 57–58
commission structure, 150
    psychic, 148
competition, dealing with the, 122–123, 129–130
confirming appointments, 45
consultative questioning techniques, 92
contacts, 84–85
creativity
    developing, 136–139, 140
    working with clients, 134–136, 141–142
customer relations, 91. 163
customers, greeting, 39–40

E

education, continuing, 54, 82
elevator pitch, 93
expectations
    company's of salespeople, 71
    coworkers' of salespeople, 72
    of company, 65–68
    of customers, 64–65
    leading to repeat business, 70–71
    of salespeople, 68–70
    one's own, 62–64

F

fear of "no," 155
Field Studies
    asking for the sale, 153
    being heard, 112
    to increase creativity, 139–140
    market research, 127
    on expectations, 72
    for sales calls, 43
    sources of contacts, 84
    the sales process, 164
    watching salespeople, 97
follow-up, 160
forms, sales forecast, 9–11

G

Guideposts for Success
    actual vs forecast sales, 27
    attitude, preparing, 52
    client awareness, 120
    company's role in success, 72
    creativity, 135

customer focus, 81
customer thoughts and mapping course, 50
expectations during sales process, 63
follow-up, 163
forecast for accountability, 26–27
keeping sales skills sharp, 151
learning, being open to 136
learning from "no," 159
lifetime value of client, 55
listening and talking, 104
listening to client, 108
maximizing opportunities, 138
networking, 83
profitable sales, 150
relationship building, 91
salesperson as product, 78
self-awareness, 127
stating differentiator, 97
success, taking the lead in own, 18–26
time management, 38–39, 41, 42

I

Information, from champion inside company, 49–50
introverts as salespeople, 114

L

lead tracking and follow-up systems, 67
listeners, types of, 108–109
listening, active ,105–108
listening skills, 111–112

M

market research, 127

N

New Traveler Tips
- account profiles, 67
- analyzing objections and problems, 164
- being heard, 112–113
- call agenda, 127–128
- closing checklist, 153
- describing self, 98
- finding creative ideas, 140
- Rule of 250, 84–85
- sales forecasts, 28
- time management, 43–44
- tracking systems, 67
- unmet expectations, 73

"no"
- fear of, 155
- learning from, 158–160

O

objections, 166–167
open-ended questions, 113

P

persistence, 94–96, 151
phone calls, managing, 80–81
Pritchett, Terry, 9–10
prospect, identifying ideal, 70

Q

qualities of successful salespeople, 66

R

referral group, 86–87
relationships with clients, 161–162
researching prospective clients, 43
responsibilities, typical sales, 36
Rule of 250, 84–85, 121

S

sale, asking for, 146–148, 155
    closing, 152–153
sales calls, 37
    confirming appointments, 45
    fundamentals of, 169
    preparing for, 41, 43, 54–55
sales coach, 82–83
sales forecast forms, 9–11, 18
sales process, 163–165
salespeople,
    compensation for, 57–58
    good habits of, 169–170
    introverts as, 114
    as product, 78
    qualities of successful, 66
    valuing the awareness of, 118–119
Seasoned Climber Challenges
    change, being prepared for, 56
    client management, 44
    communicating disconnects, 73
    open-ended questions, 113
    prospect communication derailment, 98
    researching industries, 140
sales forecasts, 28
self-assessment, 154, 165
    tending to relationships, 85

understanding of business, 128
strengths, personal, 53–54
success, taking the lead in own, 18–26
systems, lead tracking and follow-up, 67

T

technology, limitations of, 118–119
testimonials, asking for, 99–100
time forecast, 43–44
time log, 34–35
time management, 42
    "found" time, 35–36
    monitoring, 34–35, 36, 37, 43
    Sue's action plan, 38–39
tools
    account profile, 56
    call agenda, 127–128
    follow-up system, 56
    lead-tracking system, 56
    objection list, 164
    sales forecast, 19, 22–24
time forecast, 43–44
time log, 34–35

Y

you, as product, 78–79

OUR CLIENTS.
OUR HOME—RUNS.

Making it Simple, Keeping it Simple

"Change is painful. Our first meeting with The Sales Company, I recall you telling our group that they would have to provide updated sales projections and discuss them with the group every week. After the meeting, it seemed each person had some resistance to offer,"..."but we're already so busy." "...these numbers don't really mean anything because they're guesses..." Today we employ a simple and effective sales management program. Thanks to your practical approach, we have formalized our revenue forecasting process and increased individual sales accountability, thus allowing us to proactively manage our sales efforts. The new process shortly became routine. Thank you for your immeasurable help. Yes, change is painful, but mediocrity is more so."

Leaving the Competition in the Dust

The Sales Company helps you develop a successful sales strategy you can follow to results. That's been our experience. We booked 110% when our competitors were downsizing or going out of business. I know this was a direct result of the work we did with The Sales Company. They worked with us to develop a sales strategy tailored to our company and to each individual. And, they helped us stay positive and on top of the sales curve. Debbie Mrazek is great as a friend, a counselor, and adviser, but where she really excels is putting together a program that places and keeps you on top.

Making Better Decisions

We came to The Sales Company because sales were at a standstill and profits were dipping. The wisdom and perspective they brought to the sales and business side of our company were great! I never thought about sales this way before! The Sales Company continues to help us prioritize and decide which direction is best for our company. They don't make decisions for us; they help us make better decisions. My business has been steadily growing and we've hired three new employees since we started working with The Sales Company. They are the guardian angel of our business.

Focusing on What is Important

The Sales Company is a wealth of resources. Their sales coaching program provided focus for our goals and objectives. I had goals I wanted to achieve and they helped me concentrate on what was really important. They bring an abundance of business experience and understand the situational aspects of both personal and business issues. This has helped us solve challenges in an efficient, effective way. Their depth of sales and marketing knowledge, combined with strong business know-how, is a winning formula for success.

It Works!

When we first started working with The Sales Company we were sales neophytes. Their approach is to work the sales plan consistently so it's a recurring event, one that builds in accountability. It defines a process and offers tools like a tracking mechanism that moves you through a pipeline. They helped us focus not only on clients but on prospects with the highest probability of closing. It works!

Creating Best Sellers

"Creating Best Sellers—That's exactly what The Sales Company does. Your guidance in making sure I understand what the client wants, spending time questioning him or her on the value they will receive as a result of working with me is PERFECT. I was in the habit of presenting my material without adequately understanding the client's needs. It was so difficult to close or they would "have to think about it." With your approach there is no close, it just happens! Your listening to my needs and frustrations, assuring me that I can do it and helping me establish new habits has been priceless. The work we have done together has paid off over and over again. Thank you, thank you, thank you."

ORDER FORM

PRODUCTS/SERVICES	PRICE	QTY	TOTAL
HARDCOVER BOOK The Field Guide to Sales	$24.95		
eBOOK The Field Guide to Sales	$24.95		
eWORKBOOK 1 Forecasting: Your Map to Success	$27.00		
eWORKBOOK 2 Your Itinerary	$27.00		
eWORKBOOK 3 Your Backpack & Provisions	$27.00		
eWORKBOOK 4 The Landscape	$27.00		
eWORKBOOK 5 Your Traveling Companions	$27.00		
eWORKBOOK 6 Outbound Communications	$27.00		
eWORKBOOK 7 Inbound Communication	$27.00		
eWORKBOOK 8 Awareness of the Environment	$27.00		
eWORKBOOK 9 Creativity Wins the Day	$27.00		
eWORKBOOK 10 Getting What You Came For	$27.00		
eWORKBOOK 11 Overcoming Obstacles	$27.00		
eWORKBOOK 12 Just Do It	$27.00		
COMPLETE eWORKBOOK 1–12	$147.00		
COACHING	On Request		
CONSULTING	On Request		

Please fill out form and mail with your check or money order to:

The Sales Company
7325 Paul Calle Dr.
Plano, TX 75025
972-618-1880

Subtotal	
Shipping & Handling for each hardcover book: USA $5.00 International $10.00	
Tax: 8.25 % (TX residents)	
Total	

SHIP TO

NAME		
ADDRESS		APT/SUITE
CITY	STATE	ZIP CODE
EMAIL	PHONE	

www.TheFieldGuideToSales.com/Products
Debbie@The-Sales-Company.com